MW00594032

THE

PARANORMAL

RANGER

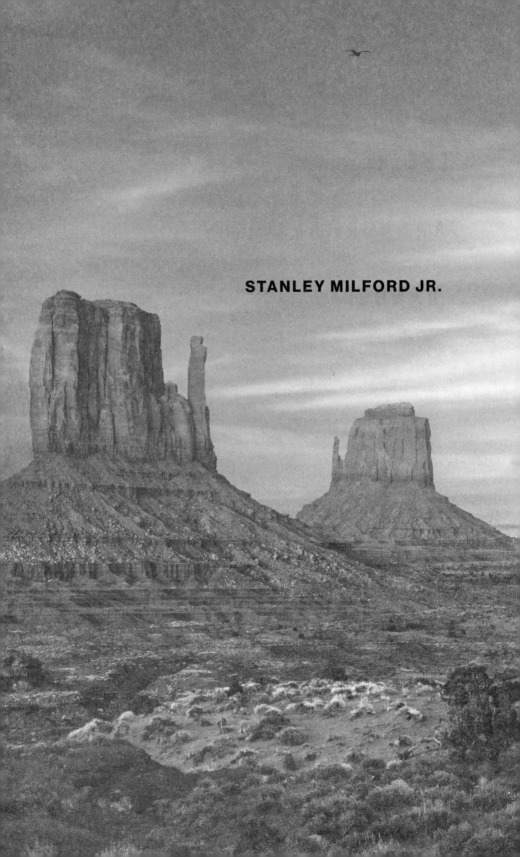

STANLEY MILFORD JR.

THE

PARANORMAL

RANGER

A NAVAJO INVESTIGATOR'S SEARCH
FOR THE UNEXPLAINED

wm

WILLIAM MORROW
An Imprint of HarperCollinsPublishers

Images in the photo insert are courtesy of the author, except:

p. 4, (*right*) Courtesy of Chris Loomis; p. 5, (*top* and *center*) Courtesy of John R. Willeto Jr.; p. 7, (*bottom*) Courtesy of Hoss Lors

HarperCollins books may be purchased for educational, business, or sales promotional use. For information, please email the Special Markets Department at SPsales@harper collins.com.

FIRST EDITION

Designed by Elina Cohen
Title page art courtesy of Shutterstock / GoodFocused

Library of Congress Cataloging-in-Publication Data

Names: Milford, Stanley, Jr., author.
Title: The paranormal ranger : a Navajo investigator's search for the
    unexplained / Stanley Milford Jr..
Description: First edition. | New York : William Morrow, an Imprint of
    HarperCollins Publishers, [2024] | Includes index. | Summary: "Former
    Navajo Ranger Stanley Milford Jr.'s chilling and clear-eyed memoir of
    his investigations into bizarre cases of the paranormal and unexplained
    over the course of his illustrious career serving the Navajo Nation"--
    Provided by publisher.
Identifiers: LCCN 2024024597 (print) | LCCN 2024024598 (ebook) | ISBN
    9780063371057 (hardcover) | ISBN 9780063371071 (epub)
Subjects: LCSH: Parapsychology—Investigation—Navajo Nation, Arizona, New
    Mexico & Utah. | Sasquatch. | Unidentified flying objects.
Classification: LCC BF1029 .M55 2024 (print) | LCC BF1029 (ebook) | DDC
    133.10973—dcundefined
LC record available at https://lccn.loc.gov/2024024597
LC ebook record available at https://lccn.loc.gov/2024024598

ISBN 978-0-06-337105-7

24 25 26 27 28 LBC 5 4 3 2 1

I dedicate this book to my mother, Emma Lorene Stacy; my father, Stanley Michael Milford Sr.; and my dear aunt, Bonnie Sue Stacy, without whom this book would not have been possible. It was their guidance, support, protection, and most importantly unconditional love that laid the groundwork for the development and creation of this book.

If you can hear me, Mom, Dad, and Bon, thank you! We did it!

I further dedicate this book to my sisters, Deborah, Stephanie, Lisa, Alex, and Margaret and to my brothers, Nathanial and Ryan, and to all of their children and family.

CONTENTS

INTRODUCTION

FOR TWENTY-ODD YEARS, I SERVED IN VARIOUS CAPACITIES AS a Navajo Ranger, including as a Ranger Sergeant and even as the delegated Chief Navajo Ranger. For eleven of those years, I was part of a team that covertly investigated reported UFOs and paranormal activity within the jurisdiction of the Navajo Reservation. After my partner, Lieutenant Jonathan Dover, officially retired, I continued to investigate the occasional case of high strangeness on a solo basis. It was after we investigated a haunting case that I had an epiphany: I had become "The Paranormal Ranger"—hence, the title of this book.

However, it was never my partner's or my intention to become investigators of the supernatural. Prior to this assignment I never expected to go looking for ghosts, Bigfoot, UFOs, extraterrestrials, Navajo witches, or skinwalkers. As a Navajo Ranger, I was thoroughly trained in all areas of law enforcement, patrol, and investigation at the US Indian Police Academy for the primary purposes of helping and protecting the public, watching over the natural resources of the Navajo Nation, and conducting investigations with an objective mind and strict adherence to protocol.

I only assumed the role and responsibility of The Paranormal Ranger after my boss saw a need on the reservation for someone to take seriously the reports of supernatural events that our communities were experiencing. My colleague Jon Dover and I were the two individuals selected for the job. Over the next decade, we investigated case after case of hauntings, unknown creatures or entities, and witchcraft. I went into each one with a simple mission: to help people. For those individuals who had experienced a paranormal encounter, it didn't matter if they were ten years old or eighty—the event could be an extremely terrifying, traumatizing, and even life-changing one. I quickly learned to shut my mouth and open my ears. My job was to listen to people, to take their concerns seriously, and to investigate their cases just as carefully as I would any other.

Despite not having volunteered for this role, I did find that I was well suited for it. I grew up in two very different worlds. One was the mainstream—and primarily Western—culture of Oklahoma, where I lived and went to school. The other was traditional Native American culture, which I received from both my mother, who was Cherokee, and my father, who was a full-blooded Navajo. I lived most of the time in Oklahoma with my mother, but the summers and holidays I spent with my father on the Navajo Reservation, where traditional beliefs and practices were a part of daily life, shaped me just as much.

This upbringing allowed me to view paranormal cases from two radically different vantage points, enabling me to approach the investigations with a balance of scientific objectivity and cultural insight.

However, this doesn't mean that the cases I investigated didn't shock or challenge or change me. Though I grew up partly in a world where sightings of both skinwalkers and UFOs were not uncommon, investigating so many paranormal cases on the Navajo Reservation brought me face-to-face with human malice, supernatural evil, and incredible mysteries I am still trying to understand to this day.

I am writing this book to share these experiences and to delve into the most fascinating cases of my career for the same reasons that I worked as a Navajo Ranger for all those years: to try to discover the truth and to help others. It is my hope to give a voice to readers who have experienced a paranormal event and to make them feel heard. I want these readers to know they are not crazy and that they are not alone.

But, of course, I want to tell my story too: my journey from a child growing up on a farm and ranch in the rural Oklahoma countryside, raised on myths and legends, to a young man who came face-to-face with the supernatural, to an experienced law enforcement officer who found a way to bridge the distance between the grim realities of modern policing and the stranger world of the paranormal.

Interspersed with my own real-life story are tales from the *Diné Bahane'*, or Navajo Emergence, which explains how the *Diné*, or Navajo, people were created. Many other Indigenous peoples have a similar origin story. This story of the Navajo people's creation was passed down from generation to generation through the centuries as an oral tradition. My own Navajo family members, including my father, paternal grandmother, many aunts, uncles, and cousins, as well as friends, passed it on to me. My account may differ from other versions you have encountered, both in structure and content; there is no official version of the Navajo creation story. Most versions agree that the creation story involves three underworlds where supernatural beings lived and supernatural and sacred events occurred that led to the forming of the Fourth World, or Shining World or Glittering World, which is where we all live today. In some stories, there are five worlds. These events happened within an area that would later be known as *Dinétah*, the center of Navajoland, which today is the ancestorial homeland to the Navajo. It was here that Changing Woman, one of the Holy People, created the four beginning clans and saved the Navajo from the monsters that would try to destroy the Navajo and the earth.

These ancient tales provide important cultural context for the cases that Jon and I worked on and offer many surprising parallels to modern-day paranormal phenomena and—I believe—some wisdom about how to understand them. Apart from these myths, all of the accounts in this book are based on actual events that occurred either in the context of my investigations as a Navajo Ranger or my own personal, firsthand experiences. These accounts are being told by me, but they also belong to the Navajo people who experienced much of the activity. The majority of these accounts come from Navajoland, the incredibly beautiful and seemingly infinite landscape I helped protect and care for throughout the duration of my law enforcement career. The Navajo Nation is the largest Native American reservation in the United States, consisting of over 27,000 square miles of diverse land that spans Arizona, New Mexico, Utah, and Colorado—roughly the size of the state of West Virginia.

As a Navajo Ranger, I patrolled tens of thousands of miles over the years, traversing the vast systems of red sandstone canyons; dense ponderosa pine forests; deep, dark caverns and caves along Marble Canyon; and the clear, icy rolling waters of the San Juan River. I have probably stood where no other person has ever stood before and heard stories that were far stranger than fiction or anything I could ever dream up. From dozens of Bigfoot sightings in the San Juan River Valley to a deeply disturbing UFO visitation near Satan Butte to a poltergeist-like haunting of an office in Window Rock, the cases I investigated led me to one inevitable conclusion: There is so much more to this world and our vast universe than we can imagine, and we have only just begun to scratch the surface.

THE FIRST WORLD

In the First World, the Diyin Dine'é, or Holy People, dwelt in darkness, without the light of Sun, Moon, or Stars. They lived on an island in the midst of deep, endless dark ocean made up of Four Seas—East, South, West, and North. The only thing that grew on the island was a Pine Tree. But the Holy People were not alone; the Insect People lived there too, as well as the two Coyotes, the Bat People, the Four Rulers of the Four Seas, and the Air-Spirit People.

Each of the four seas had its ruler. The East Sea was ruled by Big Water Creature. In the South Sea dwelled Blue Heron. The West Sea was ruled by Frog. In the North Sea, Winter Thunder ruled. Over each sea a cloud formed: a White Cloud, a Blue Cloud, a Yellow Cloud, and a Black Cloud. Within the White Cloud the Spirit of Dawn and Man dwelled. Within the Black Cloud dwelled the Spirit of Life and Woman. Blue and Yellow Cloud came together, and First Woman was formed along with yellow corn. She was beautiful and perfect in form, just like the yellow corn. White Shell, turquoise, and yucca were also formed and were with her. First Man was formed along with white corn. He too was as perfect in form as the white corn. Crystal was with First Man; it held the power of an unclouded mind and clear vision.

First Woman made a fire with her turquoise, and First Man made a fire using his crystal. This is how light was brought into the world, and the light brought First Man and First Woman together. First Man and First Woman saw each other's fires burning in the darkness of the First World and were overcome with curiosity. First Woman left her place to look for the fire in the distance belonging to First Man. First Woman's first three attempts to find the fire failed. But the fourth time she was successful and found First Man's home. First Man asked First Woman to bring her fire and to be with him, to live with First Man. First Woman agreed.

Great Coyote had grown from an egg in the water. He told First Man and First Woman that he therefore had the most wisdom; he bragged that he knew all that was under the ocean and within the sky. Just then Second Coyote, known as First Angry, appeared. He said, "You three think that you were the first beings. You are wrong. I was already here when you were formed." This saying invoked witchcraft and evil into the world.

The Air-Spirit People were overcome with anger and began to quarrel among themselves. Their conflict grew and grew, and a great fight ensued. The four rulers of the seas could stand the turmoil no more; they told First Man, First Woman, and the two Coyotes that they had to leave the First World.

First Man, First Woman, Great Coyote, Second Coyote, and the other beings had no choice but to leave the First World because of the harm they had done. So, they gathered their belongings and tools and began their long journey toward the East in search of a new home. Finally, they began climbing up through reeds toward a hole in the sky....

CHAPTER 1

A Childhood
Between Two Worlds
1976–1986

EVERY SUMMER, MY GREAT-GRANDPARENTS' HOUSE IN FORT Defiance, Arizona, on the Navajo Reservation, became the center of my world. Their house was the root from which an entire community grew, the central house in a family grouping consisting of several homes belonging to my aunts and uncles. The door was always open and there was always food and coffee waiting in the kitchen for whoever stopped by. Steeped in the smells of coffee, mutton stew, and frybread, it was where the family gathered to talk and laugh and be together, while the kids ran in and out. For a few months every summer I was one of those kids, excited to play with my many cousins and to enjoy the feeling of bustle and belonging that you can only find in a big family.

On special occasions, someone would butcher a sheep. The men would chop wood for the outdoor fire. The women would grill mutton ribs with juniper branches, to be eaten with green chile in freshly made tortillas. Inside the house, a big pot of mutton stew simmered with onions and potatoes, served with hot frybread. The sheep's intestines were made into *Ach'íí'* and its blood into blood sausage. The sheep's head would be placed directly into hot coals to singe off the wool, then brushed to remove any remaining wool. Finally, it would be wrapped in aluminum foil to bake in the oven or in a pit of hot coals—a sight that shocked me the first time I saw it, at age four or five. Later, the sheep's hide might be cleaned and used as a sheepskin rug.

Even if I only spent my summers there, the Navajo Nation was my first home. I was born in the sixties in Fort Defiance, but after my parents divorced, when I was about two years old, my mother returned to rural Oklahoma with my sister and me in tow. During the school year, I lived with my mom in Oklahoma, but almost every summer from the time I was ten years old, my sister and I boarded a plane in Tulsa and landed in Albuquerque, where my father picked us up and drove us home to the Navajo Nation, a place where we were welcomed with open arms. The sight of distant mesas, sandy arroyos, and red rock monoliths, combined with the unique and palpable scent of the red dirt and Mother Earth after the rain on the air, meant I was home.

In Fort Defiance, my father, Stanley Michael Milford Sr., was someone everyone knew and respected. He was a deeply intelligent man and an active member of his community and the Navajo Nation. He was an educator with the Bureau of Indian Affairs, worked at a number of boarding schools, taught art classes, and coached several sports. He spoke fluent Navajo, including the older dialect common among the elderly. However, it was his opinion that the English language was the path to higher education, so he did not teach me Navajo or use it when I was at home in the summers. When I first came to the Navajo

Reservation, I did try to learn the language on my own, but whenever I attempted to pronounce Navajo words, people would laugh at my "redneck" Oklahoma accent. So, after several attempts and much laughter and many tears on a little boy's part, I made the decision and deliberate refusal to ever learn the Navajo language.

My father was active in government, serving as chief of staff for the Navajo Nation, as well as campaigning for John F. Kennedy and his brother Robert F. Kennedy. My father was larger than life, practically a celebrity on the reservation: six feet tall, athletic, handsome, with a deeply likeable personality. I grew up hearing people gloat about his basketball skills, but it wasn't until he took me to a basketball tournament that I understood what they meant. During halftime, there was a free throw competition. Dad volunteered to go first and then proceeded to land one hundred free throws in a row without a single miss. That day he took home a trophy that was sticking out the car window on the way home because it was too tall to fit in the car.

I was proud of my dad and appreciated the traits that made him so popular on the reservation, but it was his deep knowledge of, and commitment to, Indigenous history that impressed itself on me the most. He had a sizable book collection and knew almost everything there was to know about Native American history. Dad taught me the history of our people and the land on which we lived, as well as the histories of other tribes. He taught me about important Native historical figures like Chief Manuelito, Chee Dodge, Geronimo, Annie Wauneka, Chief Joseph, and Sitting Bull. From him, I learned about the Cherokee's Trail of Tears, a forced march that took the Cherokee, Choctaw, Chickasaw, Seminole, and Creek tribes from their Eastern ancestral homelands to "Indian Territory"—what would later be the state of Oklahoma. I learned how the bison of the Plains tribes and other Native food sources throughout the United States were wiped out in an attempt to exterminate us. My father made sure I knew about all that Native Americans have gone through as a people, but he also emphasized our resilience, how we endured, and how we would continue to endure.

From him, I learned that my birthplace, Fort Defiance, played a pivotal role in Navajo history and was part of Navajo territory long before the US Cavalry outpost of the same name was built during the Indian Wars of the mid-1800s. This fort was built on land the Navajo had long been using for grazing their livestock. The region had witnessed a great deal of strife and conflict over the years among the Navajo, Mexicans, Utes, and then the Cavalry, whose generals initiated what was later referred to as a "scorched-earth campaign," like the strategy that was used during the Civil War. This entailed the annihilation of all crops and gardens, livestock, and natural water sources, as well as the total destruction of *hogans* (pronounced "hoe-gones"), or Navajo homes, and sometimes entire villages.

The military then proceeded to round up an estimated 10,000 Navajos and forced them to march to a reservation at Bosque Redondo—or Fort Sumner, New Mexico. Much of this march was conducted during the harsh winter months and spanned some four hundred and fifty miles, forcing them to starve or freeze to death along the way in their insufficient clothing. Many infants; small children; pregnant women; or the elderly, sick, or injured simply weren't able to endure the extremely harsh conditions and rough terrain—they died by the hundreds. Those who couldn't keep up were either shot or bayoneted to save ammunition. This forced march was later known to the Navajos as the Long Walk, an event in Navajo history comparable to that of the Holocaust suffered by the Jewish people under Hitler.

But on June 1, 1868, peace commissioners met with Navajo leaders and headmen and signed the Treaty of Bosque Redondo, or *Naal Tsoos Sani*. This treaty, also called the Navajo Treaty of 1868, allowed the Navajo to return to *Dinétah*, their Navajo ancestral homelands in what is now Arizona, New Mexico, Utah, and Colorado. The Navajo, my ancestors, walked home to Fort Defiance, where they remained. One hundred and fifty years later, on the anniversary of the Navajo Treaty's signing, I had the honor of providing security for the treaty's exhibition at the Navajo Nation Museum in Window Rock, Arizona. Touching that piece of my tribe's history and guarding its safety was one of the most profound moments of my life, both as a Navajo Ranger and a member of the Navajo Nation. Today, my tribe's history endures, but there's nothing left of the old fort at Fort Defiance. The only visible memento of the violence are a few soldiers' graves, now overgrown, uncared for, and basically forgotten.

But, of course, Navajo culture is not only history; it is also present in the day-to-day, something my father taught me by example. He still practiced many old ways and honored the traditions and taboos he learned from his own parents. For example, he taught me to dispose of my nail clippings and hair cuttings with care, not to leave them around for anyone to find. Instead, they ought to be burned so that witches couldn't use them to create curses against me. He taught me to treat elders with respect and to listen to their stories because their knowledge of our history, language, customs, and heritage would one day die with them. To this day, I consider the loss of Native and non-Native elders one of the greatest losses of the human race.

Dad was a mixture of those larger forces, the outcome of Navajo history and tradition meeting the Western world. When he was growing up, there were people on the reservation who had never encountered a white person before, and his family often traveled to the trading post to get supplies and groceries by horse and wagon. He was Navajo through and through, but he was also named for the Christian archangel Michael and the Catholic mission and school his father, Leo, helped build in St. Michaels, Arizona, near Window Rock. He attended the Catholic church and was able to hold his Christian faith hand in hand with his

Navajo heritage. He went to college at Northeastern State University, in Tahlequah, Oklahoma, and benefited from Western education and culture. But he also struggled with the same Western-caused problems of many in our community, particularly alcoholism, which often took him from the dry reservation to border towns where he could satisfy his addiction. My older sister, Deborah, and I had to go searching for him in those towns on more than one occasion.

Despite his flaws, my father was an incredibly important figure in my life, and those summers with him built up my sense of who I was and of how I fit into the world. But it wasn't only him—I spent just as much time with my grandparents, aunts, and uncles, and stayed at their houses as often as at his. In the Navajo culture, your uncles and aunts are considered your parents too. There was always someone around to look out for me and make me feel loved. In Fort Defiance, I was constantly surrounded by family, as well as by a strong sense of community and tradition.

But when I went back home to rural Oklahoma at the end of every summer, I lived in a completely different world, one ruled by Western ways and customs. Don't get me wrong—I was very happy in Oklahoma with my mother, Emma Lorene Stacy, who was of Cherokee descent. As a mama's boy, I was glad to spend most of my time with her. My mother was a loving, hardworking, active, and beautiful woman. She was often compared to the actress Natalie Wood in appearance, with her dark hair and dark brown eyes, the sort of woman people tended to admire. She was slender but strong enough to work just as hard as any man. There were times we didn't have a lot of money—and there were even times we counted pennies to buy a loaf of bread. But she made sure we never did without. She provided us with good food, a roof over our heads, and an appreciation for education. She also made our house a home, filling it with paintings and artwork, most memorably a sculpture of Venus de Milo.

My mother taught me the value of both art and beauty. Like her own mother, she always kept an immaculate home and garden with many flowers and plants. She eventually began assisting with teaching a horticulture class at a local trade school, despite not having finished high school, as she met my father when she was only seventeen. Even without a high school or college diploma, my mother was intimidatingly intelligent, creative, artistic, and well-read. She had enormous stacks of vinyl records, everything from Elvis to the Beatles to Motown to Frank Sinatra. As a kid, I was amazed at how she could sit down on the couch late at night with a three-inch-thick book and a pot of Folgers coffee, not getting up except to refill her coffee cup. She would read the entire book from front to back in one sitting. The roosters would be crowing and the sun would be on the horizon as she finished. Later, she could recite even the smallest details about what she had read.

We lived in several rural locations, mostly in and around a small farm and ranch town called Peggs, Oklahoma, a green and sunny place with Baptist churches, two grocery stores, and not much else. I had plenty of family in Oklahoma, just like on the reservation. Deborah and I were raised by three women: my mother, Emma; my maternal grandmother, Viola; and my aunt Bonnie. Mom, my grandmother, and my step-grandmother, Chloeta, were accomplished cooks. Like other Oklahomans, we ate hearty Southern-inspired food, our table always filled with fried chicken, mashed potatoes, okra, biscuits, and sweet tea. But on occasion there were traditional Cherokee foods too, such as turtle soup, boiled crawdads, fried morel mushrooms, frog legs, squirrel or rabbit dumplings, squashes, and watercress.

After my mother remarried, we lived on a farm with my stepfather Bill's family, who were also of Cherokee descent. I learned to shoot a gun and hunt by the time I was ten. I had a lot of responsibility on the farm and helped care for the cattle and sometimes milk the cows. But in my downtime, I was given free rein to explore the woods and fields and creeks, to ride my bike along the dusty dirt roads, and to go on long walks alone. I built rafts to float down a nearby creek and even walked in the woods at night. Sometimes I would go "coon huntin'" in the middle of the night with my uncles. Even as a young child, I was very close to my Creator and always felt safe from harm no matter where I went or what I did.

But in Oklahoma, despite my mother's food and stories, I was somewhat distanced from my Native identity. I went to a public school called Cherokee Elementary, but most of the students were white. I would sometimes hear about famous Cherokees like Sequoyah, who created a syllabary that made reading and writing the Cherokee language possible, or perhaps John Ross, the Cherokee chief known as the Moses of his people. But most of the culture that surrounded me was Western. In school I learned the usual curriculum of science, English reading and writing, penmanship, and arithmetic alongside the Christian religion. I often heard Native customs and beliefs called bad, evil, and wrong. I didn't agree, but I viewed the tales my parents told about shapeshifters, ghosts, and spirits as merely colorful myths or stories.

My mother's childhood was steeped in Cherokee culture and lore, passed down through generations. Her ancestors are said to have immigrated from Ireland, but by marrying into the Cherokee tribe, they were soon forced to relocate from their homelands near the Carolinas to Oklahoma Territory on the Trail of Tears. Her mother, Viola, was raised by a stern Cherokee grandmother, as her own mother had passed away when she was still very young. Viola's grandmother placed her in the Chilocco Indian Agricultural School on the Oklahoma-Kansas border to ensure that she was properly educated. My mother's father, Samuel, worked in the coal mines in Missouri as a boy and young man and later became a mercantile owner in the deep rural hills and hollows of Oklahoma, providing groceries and supplies to mostly Cherokees. There, my mother's family lived surrounded by other Cherokees, allowing her early childhood to be marked by a very strong sense of community and belonging.

But that would soon be shattered, and life as she knew it would be over. When she was only eight years old, her father died from a gunshot wound. His body was found outside of his country store, killed by a bullet from a WWII-era German Luger handgun. The authorities declared his death a suicide, but the family and neighbors were certain he had been shot in a dispute with some young men who had previously stolen gasoline from his store. Whatever the cause of his death, it effectively cut my mother off from much of her Cherokee heritage. Up until that point, she had lived in a predominantly Cherokee community, but after her father's death, her mother had to sell the store and their home and move to Tahlequah, where they lived among mostly Anglo people. Now they were isolated from Cherokee culture and community. Even so, she and her sisters had experienced enough of Cherokee culture to pass it on to me in the form of stories. One that has stayed with me all these years concerned a shapeshifter who took the form of an owl. Shapeshifters are usually considered to be out to do harm and are heavily associated with witchcraft. Understandably terrified, someone shot the owl—only to later discover a human body in its place.

I loved my mother's stories, but they seemed like something from a long-forgotten past, legends my ancestors told to shape their culture and way of life. I never discounted my mother, but I also didn't believe that the monsters she told me about were real. I was too much of a Western child for that, putting my faith in science and reason.

Even on the Navajo Reservation, surrounded by people who practiced traditional ways and depended on medicine men for their injuries, illnesses, and other troubles, who believed wholeheartedly in the dangers of witchcraft, and frequently reported supernatural sightings, I didn't fully accept the paranormal stories I heard. That was one way I was different from my Navajo cousins. There were about ten of us boys of nearly the same age who all lived near my great-grandparents' home. We had the run of that part of Fort Defiance. We were allowed to ride our bikes to the convenience store after dark, stay out past ten o'clock every night, and generally do as we pleased. My cousins were all tough, independent kids, but unlike me, they did believe these stories and took them all to heart.

One night we were all playing in the light of a full moon near the high ridge behind my great-grandparents' house when one of the cousins yelled that he saw a skinwalker running up there. No one hesitated or took time to argue as I would have done. Instead, all of the cousins scattered, running straight for the protection of home and parents. And I ran with them, caught up in the excitement and drama of the moment, even if I didn't fully understand the cause.

I had heard the tales of the *yee naaldlooshii*, or skinwalkers—shapeshifters from Navajo lore. I knew that they were reported to be bad witches who could take animal or animal-like forms in order to harm others. But it didn't register with me that these things might actually be real. It was another decade or so later, when I came face-to-face with a skinwalker myself, that I would realize how right my cousins were to run. It was only then that I would understand the stories my family members told me were not myths or make-believe.

But I had a whole childhood to live first.

Some of the most memorable times of that childhood were spent with my cousin Russell—or Rusty for short. Rusty was not quite two years older than me and much like a big brother. He and I were close growing up. His grandfather owned the Ponderosa Ranch, a cattle ranch between Welch and Peggs, which his family managed and operated, where I often stayed the night during the summers when school was on break. The ranch was a massive place of several thousand acres, full of outbuildings, tractors, fields and woods, and many winding trails and paths. Rusty and I were pretty much let loose on it to do as we liked and take care of ourselves since the adults were generally busy working and had no idea where we were. We swam in the ponds and creek, climbed trees in the forest, and played in the hay barns.

Sometimes we were daredevils. Once, when I was about eleven years old, Rusty and I took our skateboards and searched out the highest paved street in Tahlequah. We found one—a street where a residential area was about to be built. It was smooth blacktop and about a quarter-mile long, on a steep hill, maybe a twenty-five-degree angle. We walked to the very top of the hill, and I volunteered to go first. I jumped on my board and took off. God only knows how fast I was traveling when I reached the bottom of the hill! I was triumphant—until I hit a small piece of gravel and it sent me flying through the air like Superman for a good ten or so feet. I landed hard, my elbow absorbing most of the impact. I laughed through my pain and got up and dusted myself off. Rusty was laughing so hard he couldn't catch his breath. My white Fruit of the Loom T-shirt was destroyed, hanging off me in bloodied tatters. I grabbed my old blue GT skateboard, more worried about its state than my own—it was unharmed, which was all that mattered to me. We started walking back to my grandmother's house, and I threw away my shirt on the way so I wouldn't get in trouble. Back home, I superglued my wound back together, as much for fear of my dad's belt as for my own machismo.

All of these games were fun, but our favorite thing to do was play cops and robbers while riding on motocross dirt bikes. It was the era of shows like *Starsky & Hutch*, and I couldn't think of anything I'd rather be than a law enforcement officer or police detective. I consumed every police TV show I could and especially loved *Dragnet*, *S.W.A.T.*, and *Adam-12*. If there was a swaggering good guy chasing and capturing bad guys, I liked it. Rusty and I rode his dirt bikes all over the ranch, pretending to have police chases and shoot-outs. I loved the adrenaline, adventure, and thrill of catching the bad guy. I knew I was going to be a law enforcement officer when I grew up.

Fascinated by criminology, I had read about the Helter Skelter murders committed by the followers of Charles Manson in 1969. As shocking as those crimes were, they seemed far away and unreal. But I would soon encounter the same kind of brutality much closer to home. In the summer of 1977, on the morning of June 13, three little girls were found brutally murdered at Camp Scott, only ten miles from my home in Peggs. Now known as the Oklahoma Girl Scout Murders and the subject of endless media attention, including several books and documentaries, at the time it was a very real, very terrifying event for me, my family, the community, the state of Oklahoma, and the entire country. I was shocked to my core when I learned what had happened.

Camp Scott was a Girl Scout residential camp in Mayes County, just a short drive from Peggs. On the morning following their first night of camp, three girls from the Tulsa region, Lori Farmer, age eight, Michele Guse, age nine, and Doris Milner, age ten, were all found dead on a trail near their tent, their bodies left in a pile and stuffed into sleeping bags. They had been sexually assaulted, strangled, and bludgeoned to death sometime during that first night of camp. I remember the newspaper lying on the coffee table with the girls' pictures, their innocent faces smiling up from the page. They were about my age, and it was difficult to comprehend that someone could commit such a cruel and violent act upon these beloved, innocent girls.

Despite the horror of the crime, I was captivated by the manhunt that followed. Huey helicopters flew back and forth over the area, and army troop transport trucks rumbled up and down the road carrying armed posse members involved in the hunt for the perpetrator. The primary suspect, Gene Leroy Hart, a Cherokee man with a history of sexual assault and burglary who had escaped from jail in the area, remained at large for almost an entire year.

The formerly peaceful, quiet community of Peggs was plunged into chaos, shock, and terror. Deborah and I felt as frightened as everyone else. The only one not frightened was my mom, who wasn't really afraid of anything or anyone that I was aware of. One night shortly after the murders, Deborah heard something outside our house. My mom grabbed her shotgun, racked a shell in the chamber, and herded us all into the living room to sleep huddled together. We lay sleepless, listening for any hint of an intruder. Nothing more happened that night, but the effects of the Girl Scout murders on our community and way of thinking were clear. The world had changed, and even little Peggs was changing too.

Gene Leroy Hart was eventually located at the home of a medicine man and brought to trial. He was acquitted of the murders, but he still had his previous crimes to atone for and was sent to prison, where he later died while running in the prison yard at the age of thirty-five years old, apparently from a heart attack.

These events, as horrific as they were, only fueled my determination to become a law enforcement officer. I saw in the papers that detectives were trying to track down the perpetrators and bring them to justice. I realized that when I grew up, I wanted to put bad guys away and protect children like the ones whose lives had been taken for no reason. To me, to be a law enforcement officer was to be a protector, a kind of warrior who placed himself in danger in order to protect innocent lives. It was this idea that would set me on a career path from which I would never deviate. Of course, I couldn't have imagined then that my career would ever involve investigating the supernatural, but I soon had two experiences that would open my mind to all the possibilities our world contains.

When I was a teenager, my mother remarried and moved into a two-story home out of state. I stayed with my grandmother during that time to finish my high school years. On occasion I would visit my mom at her new home, where I had my first brush with the spirit world. At seventeen, I wasn't much worried about ghosts or other paranormal phenomena—I was more concerned with playing guitar and listening to music. But one night, while home alone with my younger sister, Stephanie, I would have my indifference to the supernatural tested.

My stepdad was a long-haul commercial truck driver and was often on the road for work, sometimes for weeks at a time. That night my mother was traveling with him, so it was just Stephanie and me at home. It had grown dark, and we locked the house up for the night before settling down to watch television. All of the lights in the house were turned off, except for in the living room, but suddenly I saw a faint glow emanating from the direction of the kitchen.

I was curious and got up to investigate, and to my shock I discovered that all four burners of the gas range were turned on high.

"What the hell?" I whispered to myself, darting looks around the kitchen. No one was there.

My chest tightened, and a knot formed in my stomach. I stood still for a moment, unable to do anything but stare at the glowing burners. I couldn't comprehend how the stove was lit. I knew that neither Stephanie nor I had done it, and to my knowledge there was no one else in the house. The stove was an old kind of range that still required a wooden match to light each burner, and the knobs were stiff and very hard to turn. Had someone broken into the house, crept into the kitchen, and lit the burners without me hearing or seeing them? That seemed unlikely. This couldn't be the stove malfunctioning, and this wasn't something that had happened before.

Even at that age, I tended to be calm and levelheaded in stressful and frightening situations. I tried hard to find a rational explanation. But after staring in confusion for a long, frozen moment, I couldn't find one. I turned off the burners and returned to check on my sister, who said she thought she heard something upstairs. With a feeling of unease in my belly, I went and retrieved my mom's shotgun. I checked all the downstairs exterior doors, which were locked, and then padded softly up the stairs, fully expecting to find someone hiding up there. But as I moved from room to room, and checked under the beds, in the closets, and anywhere else a person could hide, it was clear that there was no one there. Stephanie and I were alone in the house.

Or at least we were the only *living* people there.

I was perplexed, but I tried to play it off and not cause any alarm to my little sister. At the time, when I allowed myself to imagine the possibility of ghosts or spirits inhabiting the house, they didn't feel particularly menacing or dangerous. But now I did recall other past incidents and strange noises, like the time a large recliner upstairs was picked up and dropped back down with a tremendous thud. I wasn't prone to panic or hysterics, so I took it all in stride, although it started me thinking about the possibility of ghosts or spirits.

One day not long after this incident, when Stephanie and I were again home alone, I found what I can only describe as a Satanic book in the house, and I had to admit to myself that there was surely something strange going on there. I was walking down an upstairs hallway when I passed my sister's open bedroom door. Something in the room caught my eye—a huge, unfamiliar book lying on top of a gas heater, currently turned off for the warmer months. The book looked like an oversized family Bible, made of black hand-tooled leather and crumbling with age. When I picked it up, it felt like I was holding an armful of bricks. One glance made it clear this wasn't a Christian Bible—there was a large pentagram on the front.

A cold feeling spread through me, warning me this was something bad. But I opened the heavy cover anyway, and a musty, sickly smell like an old, abandoned house wafted up from the pages. What was printed on them was even worse than the smell; they contained strange, cryptic symbols and images, photographs of bizarre rituals, and other disturbing content that made me feel uneasy and nauseated. Some of the images were black-and-white etchings, and others were old color paintings. The strangest of all depicted a man's naked body with the head of a goat, an image I was sure was meant to represent Satan.

I couldn't fathom what this damn thing was doing in my little sister's room and how it came to be in her possession in the first place. I called my sister upstairs and confronted her about it. I held it up and asked her what the hell was this thing doing in her room. She said she didn't know, and that it was not hers. She said she had never seen it before. I had to admit that it didn't look new. It had clearly been well used over many years: someone had written notes in the margins in pencil and ink. This was an old tome that someone had possessed.

Now it had seemingly just appeared in our house of its own volition. Unsettled but not wanting to worry my sister further and certainly not wanting to tell my mother about it, I drove out to a friend's farm and burned the book page by page in a fifty-five-gallon trash barrel, unwilling to have its vile and noxious presence in the house. The book didn't reappear in the house, so I felt sure I had gotten rid of it and any presence that might have been attached to it.

But even then I wouldn't have called myself a believer, not really. Despite all the stories and tales I had heard growing up, I was thoroughly Western in my views of the supernatural or paranormal. I "believed" in what I could register with my five senses of seeing, hearing, touching, tasting, and smelling; and what could be proven by scientific method and logic. In just a few years, I would finally have to stop denying the reality of the paranormal.

But first I had to see a skinwalker with my own eyes.

✧ ✧ ✧

It was 1986 and I was twenty years old, spending the summer with my dad in Fort Defiance, on the Navajo Reservation. That July night, I had gone to the theater to see *Maximum Overdrive*, a horror movie based on a Stephen King novel. The soundtrack was all AC/DC, which is what had drawn me. I was a huge rock and heavy metal fan and had been playing guitar for most of my life.

The movie let out around midnight. When I walked into the lobby to dump my empty popcorn and soda containers into the trash, my eye caught on an elderly Navajo man sitting on a bench against the wall. He asked me if I was by any chance heading to Fort Defiance and could I give him a ride. He was probably in his mid-eighties, and I was surprised to see him out so late and at a Stephen King horror movie of all places, but I quickly agreed to drive him home.

We didn't talk much on the drive because the old man spoke mostly Navajo. He seemed friendly and normal, but strangely, he asked to be let out on the side of the road at the base of the hill that goes to Sawmill, Arizona—nowhere near any house that I could see. It was pitch-black out, and if there was a moon that night, I don't remember it. I left the old man in the dark and then turned the car around and drove toward my dad's house. At that time, there were few streetlights and no buildings in the area. The hospital and school hadn't been built yet. So, it was just me, my sister's car, and a long stretch of highway.

From the corner of my eye, I sensed movement out the passenger side window, like an animal running on the inside of the right-of-way fence that ran parallel to the highway. I expected to see a horse when I looked in that direction.

But what I saw made no sense. Suddenly, this thing jumped the fence, coming within three feet of the passenger side of the car. The creature was white from head to foot and ran on all fours. Its overall form appeared like that of a Greyhound, except much larger. It was about four or so feet tall to the top of its back. I couldn't tell if its feet were actually touching the ground or not. It had canine-like features, including a long snout like a dog's or wolf's. But that was where the similarity ended.

The creature was running alongside the vehicle, its speed and strength apparently limitless. It wouldn't be left behind no matter how fast I went.

Besides, I was going nearly sixty miles per hour. No animal, not even a horse, could keep up that pace. Was it even possible to outrun it? I had to try. I sped up, my hands sweating on the steering wheel, knuckles white. The speedometer climbed. Sixty, sixty-five. Seventy.

I gripped the steering wheel even harder to keep from swerving, my heart in my throat. I looked away from the road to try to get a better look at it and immediately wished I hadn't. This thing had a mouth full of long, jagged, gleaming-white teeth. It turned its head and looked straight at me. Its eyes were glowing a fiery yellow-orange, like hot burning coals glowing in the darkness—what I imagined hellfire looked like. Its lips were stretched backward in a sort of sinister grin, exposing its wicked teeth. It looked straight into my eyes like it was seeing right through me, into my soul. Its gaze was intelligent, sinister, hypnotic, and evil, and the message was clear: *I could grab you, rip you to pieces, and eat you alive, if I so chose, and there would be nothing you could do about it.* I knew in that moment that this thing was pure evil.

Drenched in a cold sweat, I slid down in my seat as far as I could while still able to see over the steering wheel and slammed the gas pedal to the floorboard. Afraid of what I might see, I didn't look in the direction of the creature again, and I deliberately didn't look in my rearview mirror. I had realized that whatever this was, it was a predator—and in that moment, I was its prey. The only thing I could do was to get as far away from it as quickly as I could.

The next thing I remember is sliding into the gravel driveway outside my dad's house and running inside, slamming the door behind me. My dad looked up in surprise and asked what was wrong. Breathlessly, I told him my experience. He nodded sagely, not a hint of disbelief on his face, and said the words I already knew in my heart: "Son, you just saw a skinwalker."

I, of course, knew what a skinwalker was. My dad and other relatives had talked about them throughout my life. But I never expected to encounter one myself. I tried to wrap my mind around what this meant—that I had seen and been chased by a skinwalker. The one concrete thought I could form in that moment was *Holy shit . . . this is real!*

Later, when I shared what had happened with my Navajo relatives, no one was surprised. Some of them suspected that the elderly man I had picked up at the movie theater was responsible. It was certainly a possibility, considering the strangeness of his presence at the theater so late at night and his wish to be dropped off in such a remote place, but he had given me no indication that he held any malice toward me.

Besides, my concerns were much larger than one old man. My entire worldview had been challenged. All of the myths and legends, every story my parents, aunts and uncles, grandparents, cousins, and neighbors had told me—of shapeshifters and ghosts and UFOs—suddenly loomed up in a brand-new light, full of terrifying possibility. What if some of it was actually real, like the skinwalker—the owl shapeshifter, the UFOs on the reservation, the work of the medicine men, the presence in my mother's home? My chest tightened as I remembered each of them. I had to consider the possibility that at least *some* of them weren't make-believe, weren't fairy tales, weren't myths better left in the past to collect dust. What if some of those stories were part of everyday reality, glimpses into a wider, stranger world that most Westerners were either unaware of or simply chose to ignore?

Seeing the skinwalker was an awakening. My mind had been opened. The world teemed with possibilities. No matter how skeptical or scientific my nature, I could never entirely go back to not believing. I would always have to ask, *What if?*

What if monsters were real?

THE SECOND WORLD

First Man, First Woman, Coyote, Coyote First Angry, and the other beings crawled up through the hole they'd found in the sky and emerged into a world where everything was blue. They had reached the Second World. There was a vast Blue Plain, with blue cone-shaped houses scattered all around. This World was inhabited by Blue Furred Mammals, all of whom were blue and gray in color. This was a world of wings and songs, with bluebirds, blue jays, blue hawks, and blue herons in great numbers. Táshchozhii, Swallow Chief, was the ruler here.

The Air-Spirit People, or Newly Arrived People, were treated with kindness and respect. The Swallow People and Swallow Chief said, "You are welcome to stay here with us." The Swallow People offered their Blue World to be the Air-Spirit People's new home and were willing to live together with them.

Life among the Swallow People and the Air-Spirit People was good for a time. They had even begun addressing one another as family members: Brother, Sister, Father, Mother, Son, and Daughter. They treated one another as one tribe and one people.

But the Newly Arrived People were not quite content with their new family. They sent two scouts called Locust and White Locust out into the East of the Blue World to see if they could find people like themselves. Two days later, Locust and White Locust returned after reaching the edge of the World. Their journey was fruitless, as they never found any people or even animals or plants—no sage, no pine trees or grass, not even mountains. The Blue World was barren and uninhabited by beings or people of any kind.

Again, the Locusts were sent out, this time to the South. When they returned, they stated all they discovered was great, open, barren land. No people, no animals, trees, plants, water, or food. The Locusts continued their scouting to the West, then finally to the North. They never found anyone or anything.

The Swallow People soon learned the Air-Spirit People had sent scouts to each of the four directions to the edge of the Earth. The Swallow People came to the Newly Arrived People and asked why they had sent scouts out into the Blue World. The Newly Arrived People stated they did so because they were unfamiliar with the Blue World and had sent the scouts to determine if there were people like themselves; to see what the land was like; and to see if there were any plants, animals, trees, mountains, water, or food.

Even though the Air-Spirit People, or Newly Arrived People, had been welcomed as family into a new home in the Blue World and been given fellowship and a great many gifts and blessings, they still had not changed their bad ways of living and were not living in *hózhó*—harmony, peace, and balance. One of the Air-Spirit People had secretly committed adultery with the Swallow Chief's Wife. When the Swallow Chief learned of this he came to the Air-Spirit People and said, "We, the Swallow People, welcomed you and your people into our World. We treated you like family. We gave you all that we had to give—food, shelter, and clothing. Now, because of your transgressions, you are no longer welcome in the Blue World. Now you must go. You are to leave this World now and never return...."

CHAPTER 2

A Navajo Ranger in the Making

1997–2000

MY CHILDHOOD DREAM OF BECOMING A LAW ENFORCEMENT officer never left me; that little boy who played *Starsky & Hutch* on the Ponderosa Ranch grew up into a young man with a deep desire to help people and serve his community in a meaningful way. So, when I was offered the chance to become a Navajo Ranger, I immediately accepted, as excited as an adult as my childhood self would have been. I had been working in construction and security for the Parks and Recreation Department in the summers while I was attending college in Kansas. I had been accepted to the University of Arizona and had started school there when one of the founding Navajo Rangers, Clarence Gorman, who was then the Director of Parks and Recreation, contacted me and advised that a ranger was needed for Monument Valley. He asked if I would return to the Navajo Nation to work as a Navajo Ranger. My mother was thrilled and proud of me, but my father was less supportive, despite having family members who were police officers. His drinking habit had made him disdainful of the police, and his politics were at odds with government law enforcement. He didn't say anything outright, but I knew he was critical of my decision.

I was to be commissioned as a Navajo Ranger, but my salary would be funded by the Navajo Nation Parks and Recreation Department. I verbally agreed to attend the police academy and come back to work as a park ranger at Monument Valley, in Arizona and Utah. I had some grueling months ahead of me, but I knew it would all be worthwhile once I received my badge and gun and began my law enforcement career. But only a month before I was to start my police academy training, when I was thirty-one years old, the worst thing I could imagine happened.

My mother died.

The doctors said it was a heart attack, the result of a blocked artery. The entire family was shocked because there had been no warning signs. Mom was only in her fifties. She was slim and active and always seemed strong and healthy, but like many people from that part of the country during that time period—when even my junior high school had a designated student smoking area—she was a smoker. It happened one day as she was doing yardwork, as she often did, even in hundred-degree heat. My Aunt Lois and my cousin Jennifer were visiting from Arkansas at the time, and my Aunt Lois had told my mom to come inside because it was too hot outside. But my mom, who could be stubborn, waved her concern off, saying that she would be okay. My youngest sister, Lisa, who was fourteen at the time, remembers that as she was leaving the house, Mom had been trimming the hedge in the front yard and she had seemed completely fine.

Later that day, Lisa called and asked to speak to Mom, and when Aunt Lois went into the bedroom to get her, Mom didn't respond. So

Aunt Lois shook her and found that the heel of my mother's foot was cold to the touch. She turned the light on and found Mom slumped across the bed, as though she had fallen, and one of her shoes was on the floor. Aunt Lois yelled out that something was wrong with Mom, and that someone should call for an ambulance. Since Mom was not breathing, Jennifer and a family friend named Shirley began CPR on her and continued until the EMTs arrived and took over. They shocked her heart five times before it started beating again.

But at the hospital, my sister Steph, who had been working in the medical field for two years, learned from the doctors that one of Mom's eyes wasn't responding to light, which meant that Mom likely had very serious brain damage. She knew Mom wouldn't recover. But the hospital still decided to fly Mom to a better hospital in Tulsa.

When I arrived at the hospital in Tulsa, I sat by my mother's bed and spoke to her, and sometimes she would squeeze my hand as if in response. But in the end, the damage was too great, and my mother passed away. Her death hit us like a semitruck. One moment she was there, and the next she was gone.

I was devastated. I had seen her briefly that summer while traveling with my dad and girlfriend on our way to Kansas, where my father was to attend a college graduation. It had been a little while since I'd visited my mom, and we were really enjoying being together. My girlfriend and I had hoped to stay longer in Oklahoma while my dad continued on to Kansas, but he pulled a guilt trip on me, threatening to drink if I left him alone. Knowing how he behaved while drinking, I didn't want to risk leaving him to his own devices. So, I said goodbye to my mom and went to Kansas, unaware that it was the last time I would ever see her. After I learned of her death, I was consumed with anger at my father. I thought if he hadn't pushed me to leave, I might have been with my mom long enough to notice she was having a health issue and would have made her go to the doctor. Maybe if I had, she would still be here today.

I know now that that isn't true. My sister Steph recently told me that the ER doctor had explained to her that my mother's death was really a fluke incident. He said that a piece of plaque had dislodged in one of her arteries and had blocked the artery, stopping blood flow to her heart and causing her to have a heart attack. He said most of the time when plaque breaks off like this it will simply pass on through, but this time it had lodged and blocked the blood flow. He said that, in fact, Mom's heart was actually in good condition considering her age and the fact that she lived on cigarettes and coffee. He said the truth was, even if she had been in the emergency room at the time of the incident the outcome probably would have been the same.

But I didn't know any of that then, and I'm not sure it would have helped. I had a world of grief ahead of me.

IN 1997, I entered the United States Indian Police Academy at the Federal Law Enforcement Training Center in Artesia, New Mexico. All of the cadets came from various Native American law enforcement departments, representing federally recognized tribes from around the United States—Navajos and Hopis from the Southwest, Utes from Colorado, and Natives from several tribes in the East. There was a camaraderie among the cadets based on the bond of our shared Indigenous identity. The conversation around me was familiar, even though the other cadets came from different tribes. We shared many cultural similarities that made talking to one another easy. As we ate the standard American fare in the mess hall, our thoughts would turn to the hot frybread, tortillas, and mutton stew back home. On the weekends in the barracks, you could hear powwow and ceremonial music playing, which made the academy feel a little more like home. It was easy to be together; we soon grew into a brotherhood.

The Indian Police Academy was designed to be quasi-military, kind of like a civilian police boot camp. Sergeants oversaw all aspects of the training, teaching the law enforcement related courses, marching and parade drills, and the daily physical training. The sergeants were basically drill instructors like you see in the Army or Marines with their high-and-tight military haircuts, starched and pressed uniforms, and their campaign hats angled downward with the brim just above the eyebrow. All of my sergeants were prior military, highly trained in SWAT, and frequently served on special task forces. Their skill sets and services were in such high demand that Blackhawk helicopters would sometimes come swooping into the academy to fly them off to help with hostage situations and other crises on sovereign Indian lands, where tribes are responsible for handling their own situations and sometimes request the Bureau of Indian Affairs's assistance.

Upon our arrival, the sergeants were true gentlemen, so friendly and accommodating, much like concierges at a five-star resort. They were all smiles and courtesy as they helped us get settled in. But once we had let down our guard, they deployed a grenade—literally. It was a "flashbang," also known as a flash sound device (FSD), basically a stun grenade. But the sound pressure and deafening blast sent cadets flying. Some were flat on the ground, some were running, some were screaming, and some were crawling home. Over this mass of chaos, a thundering voice arose like that of Charlton Heston as Moses, only with very colorful, profanity-laced vocabulary: "Shut up, you maggots! Get in formation, you sorry dirtbags!"

Everyone was running and scrambling to get into this thing called formation, only we had no idea what formation was supposed to be. It looked like a scene from *Keystone Cops* or *The Three Stooges*, only with fifty-plus stooges. Once the sergeants grabbed us and organized us into something resembling a formation, one sergeant yelled, "Drop! Front lean and rest position!"

We dropped into the required push-up, and there was an instant collective cry of pain, which soon gave way to anguished moaning. They had dropped us facedown to do push-ups in a field of bull-head thorns. It was like grabbing two handfuls of pushpins and tacks and squeezing hard. As we did push-up after push-up, the thorns leached their toxins into our skin, stinging and burning. When I risked a glance at the sergeants, I saw their friendly smiles had dissolved into mischievous grins.

The first week of training, affectionately known as Hell Week, seemed to be the longest week of my life. But even after it was over, our suffering didn't end. Sometimes the sergeants would sneak into our rooms and wake us with a blaring whistle or an eardrum-shattering air horn or by simply yelling at the top of their lungs. During room inspections, everything had to be exact and almost perfect, free of mess and dirt. Even the commode had to sparkle like brand new. They couldn't so much as find dust in the vents on the air conditioner. Some sergeants would come to room inspections wearing a pair of white military dress gloves and carrying a ruler to conduct their morning inspection. The sheets on the bed had to be so tight and folded so exactly that the sergeant could bounce a quarter off the bed. If any part of the bed was even slightly incorrect, they would rip all the linens off and throw them on the floor, demanding that you start over. All clothing had to be pressed, folded, and put away perfectly. Boots and shoes had to be immaculately shined so that the sergeants could see themselves in the reflection.

I was so desperate to avoid censure that I would secretly iron my towels, sheets, and socks before I put them away. With this kind of attention to detail, I always passed the inspections with flying colors. Sometimes, I think this would annoy some of my sergeants, because they usually couldn't find anything out of place on my side of the room. On one memorable morning, a sergeant inspected my room as usual, then he went back over it. I was standing at attention, beaming with pride because he couldn't find any discrepancies.

Then, all of a sudden, he yelled out, "Cadet Milford, front and center!" At the police academy, every command was barked out in typical drill instructor fashion: deep, gruff, often about an inch from your face, and usually loud enough to damage your hearing. I had gotten used to it, but this time, I flinched in surprise. I was sure I had everything squared away.

I ran from being at attention to where the sergeant was standing by a mirror. I replied, "Yes, Sergeant!"

He said, "What the hell is that on my mirror, Cadet Milford?"

I glanced up at the mirror and sure enough, right there in the center of what had been, only moments earlier, a sparkling clean mirror, was a huge, nasty fingerprint.

"It appears to be a fingerprint, Sergeant!" I replied.

"What the hell is a damn fingerprint doing on my mirror, Cadet Milford?"

"I do not know, Sergeant!"

"Cadet Milford, do you not know how to clean a damn mirror?"

"Yes, Sergeant!"

"Yes, what?"

"Yes, I do know how to clean a mirror, Sergeant!"

"Cadet Milford, apparently you don't!"

"Yes, Sergeant!"

"Cadet Milford, drop and give me fifty!"

"Yes, Sergeant!" I dropped and knocked out fifty push-ups as fast as I could and got back in formation.

Because my sergeant couldn't find anything out of order, he had taken off his glove and smudged his thumbprint on my mirror. I learned that day that if they wanted to get you, they would find a way.

Now, when I look back on my months at the Indian Police Academy, I can laugh at how hard it was. But there was a shadow cast over my time there too, my mother's death hanging over me like a heavy black veil, as well as my anger at my father. I was still traumatized by her death and so numb that it was impossible for anyone to push my buttons. I was hurting so much on the inside that there was nothing the sergeants or anyone else could do to make me feel worse. The pain of doing push-ups in a field of bullheads or on frozen blacktop couldn't begin to compare to the agony I felt inside.

Yet through that numbness, there was a deep desire to make my mother proud. I knew that even though she was gone, she was still watching over me. Instead of letting her sudden passing destroy me, I turned it around and took all the great memories I had of her and let them drive me to do the very best I could at everything. When we ran or did any kind of physical training, I let her memory push me through the pain, to run faster and train harder. She had been so proud when she learned that I was accepted to the police academy, and I wanted to be worthy of that pride. Still, there were nights I lay awake in the dark staring at the ceiling with a river of tears flowing from my eyes, thinking about her. I missed her terribly, but in some ways, the high intensity of the police academy helped me to get through the worst of the pain of her loss, as well as the anger I felt at my father.

Despite the death of my mother and the extreme difficulties of training, I found it easy to thrive at the academy. I figured out quickly that the sergeants were simply trying to filter out the people who had no business wearing a badge and carrying a gun. Those who had to question everything, complain about everything, or always get the last word weren't cut out to be law enforcement officers and they didn't last long. Our class started out with about fifty cadets, but only half of us made it to graduation. From the police academy, I learned that succeeding in law enforcement meant doing what you were told, no matter how strange or unpleasant your orders.

From the academy, I also acquired an attention to detail that would stay with me, not only for the rest of my career but for the rest of my life, becoming a part of my being and identity. In the academy, they taught you not to take shortcuts. Whether you were working on paperwork or your own personal appearance, you could leave no detail unattended. This habit has served me well in the many cases I've investigated, paranormal ones included. The academy taught me that the career I was entering into wasn't going to be easy, and that as a law enforcement officer, I would be held to a higher standard than everyone else. It was now my duty to help and protect the public, and this would mean being vigilant in the extreme. The sergeants drilled this habit into us by constantly sneaking up on us when we were in conversation or distracted with another task and trying to steal our aluminizers, simulated handguns made of solid aluminum. The simulated gun may not have been real, but if a sergeant succeeded in taking it away from you, it meant you were in serious trouble. It was an effective way to teach us to be alert at all times, and it drove home the unique role I would play as a Navajo Ranger and the weighty responsibility I would carry every time I put on my uniform and went to work.

I took every lesson to heart. Though I wasn't the number one cadet, I did graduate with a few honors, one for my shooting skills and the other in the Physical Efficiency Battery, or PEB. The PEB was a series of physical tests that included running a timed mile and a half, weightlifting, and flexibility testing. I had the honor of serving as the platoon leader and graduated as the first squad leader, for which I also received an award. By the end of my time at the police academy, it was clear to me that I had chosen the right career path—one I was not only excited about but also well suited for.

It was a time of celebration and pride for me. Members on both sides of my family attended my police academy graduation, and though I felt my mother's absence keenly, I also felt surrounded by my family's and community's love and support and knew that my mother was watching over me with pride in her heart.

Immediately after I graduated from the academy, I came home to begin my field training. For the Navajo Rangers, this is when a rookie officer learns standard operating procedures and how not to get killed while patrolling. The rookie is supervised and assessed by an experienced and seasoned field training officer from various law enforcement and natural resource enforcement departments, such as the Navajo Police, Fish and Wildlife, Forestry, Archaeology, Animal Control, and the Environmental Protection Agency.

After completing this intradepartmental ride-along field training, I was officially a Navajo Ranger, ready to begin patrolling the vast reservation and serving the public. As I climbed into my patrol unit—a four-wheel-drive pickup truck—on my first morning flying solo, I realized that I had arrived. After all these years, my childhood dreams from the days of playing cops and robbers with my cousin Rusty had been realized. I had *made it*. I was now a commissioned law enforcement officer—a Navajo Ranger.

Initially, I was assigned to work in Shiprock, New Mexico, where it seemed like I performed thousands and thousands of livestock inspections. The livestock industry is one of the primary—if not *the* main source—of income and economic security for the Navajo people. In general, livestock inspections and proof of ownership are required to sell or transport any livestock. Rangers and livestock inspectors are the individuals responsible for the inspections. I remember mile-long lines of livestock trailers disappearing into the distance, with customers yelling in Navajo because I was not working fast enough. Each individual animal, which included cows, sheep, horses, and other livestock, had to be inspected from head to toe, and their description had to be handwritten on an inspection form, a tedious process performed in the blazing desert heat.

Mercifully, after a few months, I was reassigned to Monument Valley as was originally planned, where I did my best to get the hang of the whole cop thing. My first days of policing were filled with drunks and DUIs, domestic violence calls, traffic enforcement, and bootlegging and alcohol violations. After putting the local troublemakers behind bars a few times, things started to settle down. I began working closely with the local Navajo Police, the various local sheriff deputies, National Park Service Rangers, and my fellow Navajo Rangers to learn everything I could about what it meant to be a law enforcement officer. My time as a recruit may have lasted only one year, but in reality, it takes years to fully train as a Navajo Ranger—to get a feel for everything you need to know to do your job safely and well, and to be able to handle anything thrown at you in the line of duty. But I still had a lot of learning to do about what it meant to be a Navajo Ranger.

The Navajo Rangers were founded in 1957 by Richard Van Valkenburg, an archaeologist who worked for the Navajo Nation Archaeology Department. Van Valkenburg envisioned a law enforcement department very much like that of the National Park Service Rangers. The Navajo Rangers would protect the archaeological resources on the reservation and in the park areas. They must additionally be skilled in interpretation and as park guides, much like rangers at Yosemite and the Grand Canyon, or closer to home, the Canyon de Chelly at the heart of Navajoland.

The Navajo Rangers were specifically designed to deal with the tourism boom on the Navajo Reservation that had followed the release of major motion picture films by John Ford with John Wayne as the star, such as *Stagecoach* (1939), *Fort Apache* (1948), and *She Wore a Yellow Ribbon* (1949). These movies resulted in modern highway systems that for the first time allowed people from outside to visit the Navajo Reservation. People were arriving in increasingly large numbers to see Monument Valley, Canyon de Chelly, and other beautiful natural features in the area. Thus, the Navajo Nation desperately needed a law enforcement department that could protect the natural and archaeological resources people were so eager to see—the pictographs painted on rock, the petroglyphs carved in red sandstone, and the Anasazi ruins found in Canyon de Chelly and other areas.

The majority of the 27,000 square miles of the Navajo Nation is actually made up of archaeological ruins. Almost everywhere you go, there are artifacts that show people have lived in the area for thousands of years. For example, in Utah, the Fremont culture left behind images of people, animals, and geometric shapes in the red rock throughout the canyons. These images tell stories of their histories, mythologies, and cultural preoccupations. Other cultures like the Hopi and Pueblo did the same. The Navajo Rangers were tasked with protecting these ancient depictions and artifacts, alongside our natural resources like forests and waterways. That protection is essential because once an artifact, such as a clay vessel or pot, is destroyed or stolen, the information and history associated with that item is then erased, gone forever. All future people, not only Indigenous ones, lose out on that piece of cultural history.

Before long, the Navajo Rangers expanded its focus beyond archaeological concerns and became a catch-all agency, providing enforcement of timber, fish, and game, as well as enforcing the criminal code. There is no other law enforcement agency in the United States—

maybe even worldwide—that provides such a wide spectrum of services over such a vast area of terrain. Besides, the Rangers are few in number. At the start of my career, there were about forty Rangers, but by the time I left, there were only eight remaining. It is a great deal of responsibility for such a small number of people. Thus, the Navajo Rangers also require a great deal of training in many different areas, ranging from forestry to animal control to livestock inspections to archaeological law. My partner, Jonathan Dover, once estimated that he had undergone 4,000 hours of training in the course of his career.

The difference between being a typical police officer and being a Navajo Ranger is something like the difference between being a doctor and being a medicine man. A Western doctor treats a patient's specific symptoms and sends them home, but a Navajo medicine man takes a more holistic approach. He wants to bring the patient back into balance, bring their entire life into harmony. In the same way, I wanted to bring the individuals I encountered into balance with their surroundings and community. I found it far more effective to take time to talk to offenders and help them understand the reasons for the laws they had broken and what the consequences might be rather than simply issuing tickets. For example, if someone was speeding, I would explain the reason for the speed limit in the area and tell them about the fatal accidents that had occurred there due to difficult terrain, weather conditions, and driver carelessness. Overall, I found that treating people like fellow human beings instead of being badge-heavy always resulted in more compliance. I was a member of the community, and that's how I conducted myself while on the job.

Every day, I did my best to look at the big picture and consider what I was trying to accomplish in my community. It was important to me to be a positive force in people's lives. Once, I had to deal with a family in the north of the reservation that was embroiled in a dispute over land ownership rights. Tensions had mounted so high that they were actually shooting at one another over supposed trespassing. The situation was steadily escalating, and I was afraid someone was going to get hurt or killed, which was not an uncommon outcome of these kinds of disputes on the Navajo Reservation. One day, as I was driving down a dirt road in the area while on patrol, my sixth sense warned me to stop the truck. When I got out, I discovered that someone had buried a board with six-inch square-head nails sticking up—an attempt by one half of the family to keep the other half off the land.

In law enforcement, an officer quickly comes to rely on their intuition, inner voice, gut instinct, or what I like to call "sixth sense." By sixth sense, I mean the human perception of unseen stimuli beyond our commonly recognized five senses of hearing, seeing, touching, smelling, and tasting. It is a precognition of something bad that is going to happen. Some individuals think of this as a supernatural ability or power that has been gifted by the Creator. Some think of this as a skill that has been learned or worked at. For me, I think it is a mix of all the above. This sense keeps law enforcement officers safe on a daily basis, and for some it may have even saved their lives at some point. Throughout my entire career as a Navajo Ranger, this sixth sense proved to be my guardian spirit on many occasions.

When I found that nail-riddled board, I knew it was time to intervene. I arranged a mediation with the feuding family members at a local chapter meeting. About a hundred people turned up, as it was a huge family. I attempted to mediate their dispute, along with members from the chapter. At first, there was a lot of chaos and yelling, but I finally got them under control and made them take turns sharing their sides. It took several hours for everyone to make their case. By the end of the meeting, they were crying and hugging and saying they were sorry. Instead of putting somebody in jail, I instead worked hard to bring the families together and heal the community. This is what being a Navajo Ranger is all about.

It was certainly not a glamorous job, but it was often very rewarding. One of my favorite memories from my rookie days is the time I rescued a goat. I was fresh out of the police academy when I was called to the home of an elderly Navajo man in a remote area south of Lake Powell. He was in tears because his goat had climbed out on a huge rock formation and was stuck on a sheer cliff with a thousand-foot drop. The goat had been out there for nearly two days.

You have to understand that on the Navajo Reservation, especially among the elderly, people's livestock are often their entire financial safety net, and sometimes even their entire source of income. Often, the elderly end up completely alone in remote areas, with only their livestock for companionship. The animals can become like family to them, so for both financial and personal reasons, livestock is very highly valued. That was absolutely the case with this man, who was in his eighties and lived all alone. His goat was like a family member to him.

I was determined to retrieve the goat and put the old man's mind at ease. I hiked out to the rock formation and assessed the situation. Luckily, I had extensive rock-climbing experience, so I knew exactly what to do. Carefully, I climbed out to the goat and put a rope around it before working my way back off the cliff and pulling the animal to safety. When I returned the goat to the old man, you would think I had rescued his own child from certain death. He was so happy to have the goat home safe that he hugged me again and again.

I felt a great sense of accomplishment in being able to return the man's goat. It was only when I had driven back down and looked up at the spot where I'd found the goat that I realized exactly how high up I had been and how dangerous the rescue actually was. However, it was well worth the risk to me to help the old man, and I felt that putting my life in danger was simply part of what it meant to be a law enforcement officer. I had faith in my Creator and believed that if I lost my life while serving and protecting the public, then it was simply meant to be.

Danger was, in fact, a constant and inescapable part of the job. Navajo Rangers work in extremely remote areas where backup can be an hour and a half away. Rangers must rely on their experience and intuition, trusting their training and sixth sense to let them know when they need to back out of a situation and wait for help. I had to learn very early on not to paint myself into a corner and to always have a way out. For example, if I was hiking into a ruins site where armed looters were present, I needed to know when to retreat and call for backup. When a single Anasazi vessel could be sold for over $40,000 on the black market, the looters would be willing to shoot anyone who got in their way. If they got caught, they would go to prison for a long time, so they wouldn't back down from a fight. This could create very dangerous situations.

Monument Valley, the area that was truly my first beat, was a place a law enforcement officer needed to be careful. Ten years before I became a ranger, just west of Monument Valley, two Navajo Police officers, Roy Lee Stanley and Andy Begay, had responded to a call of individuals partying and drinking. Roy was the first to arrive; the partyers assaulted him, tied him up, and shot him. Later, Andy arrived only to suffer the same fate. They put the two wounded officers in their patrol units, doused them with gasoline, and set them on fire. Even though both of the officers had been shot, their gunshot wounds were not fatal. Autopsies revealed that there was soot in their lungs, which meant they had breathed in the smoke as they died. Horrifically, both officers had burned alive in their patrol units.

I thought of those two officers often, especially when I patrolled in the Chuska Mountains, where there were many lakes, including Wheatfields, Asaayi, Whiskey, Todacheene, and Berland. The area had a lot of natural resources and many recreation spots that were frequented by both locals and tourists. Recreation spots meant partying, and partying meant drinking, which is illegal on the Navajo Reservation. Alcohol and substance abuse were frequent problems in the area, with repeat offenders I would have to take to jail over and over again.

Traffic-wise, Monument Valley was also a perfect storm for disaster. To start with, there were tons of locals driving what are known on the Navajo Reservation as "rez rockets," a term used to describe an old junk Indian car. Usually, it was loud, beat-up, and had rust or primer paint or a combination of the two as the primary color. The windshield was cracked and the windows were knocked out. None of the tires matched and all of them were bald. It had bailing wire or duct tape holding an expired license plate on—if there was one at all. There was usually an eagle feather hanging from the rearview mirror, a prayer to hold everything together. If I heard what sounded like a gunshot, most of the time it was a rez rocket backfiring.

So, there were lots of people driving these rez rockets, often while under the influence, plus visitors from places like Europe with their Jaguars, Maseratis, or Ferraris doing 115 miles per hour, and retired elderly folks with their nine-foot-wide, forty-foot-long rock-star tour buses clogging up the roads. Added to this already chaotic mix were "coyotes"—human traffickers or smugglers—transporting van loads of undocumented migrants like cords of wood, and livestock owners who allowed their livestock to graze in the right-of-way. It was a deadly mix I had to face every single day.

But people weren't the only—or even the main—point of concern. The landscape itself was treacherous, full of sudden drops that could send you off a cliff, wind and snowstorms that would come up quickly, and animals that could tear you apart or stop your heart with their venom: bears, mountain lions, bobcats, rattlesnakes, and scorpions. Even a severely sprained ankle had the potential to turn into a fatal event in such a remote place. I was determined to know the terrain as well as possible, so I would fuel up my truck in the morning and drive up into the mountains, where I deliberately would try to get lost, finding my way out through logging roads and goat trails. This was the best way to learn the terrain and avoid falling prey to its more dangerous elements.

Despite the danger, there was immense beauty and satisfaction in the job. There were experiences I can only describe as magical. Being out in the remote reaches of Navajoland at night was one of the most intense experiences of my life. There was very little ambient light from the nearby communities and residential areas, so the stars were brighter than most people today can imagine. They seemed so close and bright; it was almost like you could reach out and touch them. The Milky Way was clear and vivid in the sky, utterly breathtaking. The nighttime sky seemed to have its own personality and character. For the first time, I understood how the Navajo creation stories had come to be thousands of years ago. Looking up at those stars, it was easy to imagine how they had led early Navajo and other tribes to tell stories about the creation of the world and about Star People, visitors from the sky, whether gods or extraterrestrials. It was impossible not to ponder the creation of the world and the limits of the universe while out patrolling the vast, remote regions of the Navajo Nation.

I had been taught by my father and my Navajo family to respect the land because everything in our world has a spirit, whether rock or tree or river. Out in the quiet wilderness, I felt their spirits and the life inside them. I felt how much the natural world was owed my deep respect. As I watched elk, coyotes, prairie dogs, and eagles go about their lives, at times I felt a deep connection to them and to my Creator. When I'd sit at the crest of a sand dune, admiring the soft and flowing lines of the sand and listening to the warm desert wind whispering through the sunbaked canyon, I felt the earth itself speak to me of time and space. I felt tied to everything around me, all that had come before and would come after.

I loved the remoteness and vastness of the reservation, and I understood why so many non-Native people traveled so far for a glimpse of it. Thus, I never begrudged the tourists who came to see and understand Navajoland. In fact, I genuinely enjoyed working with the visitors who came to Monument Valley from all over the world. Once, a group of two hundred students from Holland, all girls ages eight to fourteen or so, were visiting Monument Valley on a school trip. They had begun setting up their tents for the night when a severe windstorm came up very quickly, blasting them with stinging sand. They were running around screaming in terror. It was like herding cats, but we finally got them all safe inside a nearby warehouse, where they rolled out their sleeping bags and set up their camp chairs.

All of the girls understood English, as most people in Holland do, so I took the role of storyteller, telling them stories I had learned from my father. They were especially captivated by tales of the Long Walk and about the Navajo chief Chee Dodge, who learned to speak English as a little boy and worked as an interpreter during and after the Long Walk, helping the elderly Navajo understand what the government agents and soldiers were saying at Fort Defiance when they came for their rations. The girls were captivated; as the wind finally calmed, you could hear a pin drop in the room. As I spoke, I thought about the long line of Navajo who had lived between worlds and used that unique position to change things in the Navajo Nation. I saw a line spanning from Chee Dodge to my father to myself. I was part of a long chain of Navajo who stood with a foot in each world.

Long before Jon Dover and I were tasked with investigating paranormal cases in an official capacity, the paranormal sometimes intruded on my life as a Navajo Ranger. It was impossible for it not to in a place like Navajoland, where so many practiced the old ways. But there was one particular instance during my rookie days that stayed with me and made me realize that patrolling the Navajo Nation would involve far stranger cases than I had imagined when I first signed up for the job.

I was called out to a small community on the south side of the reservation in Arizona. A veterinarian had responded to a call regarding twenty-six sheep that had been killed. When the vet was unable to find a cause for the deaths, he called the Navajo Rangers to investigate. Livestock deaths were not an uncommon occurrence on the reservation, as livestock are plentiful and attacks by predators and even domestic or feral dogs are bound to happen. But as I drove up the road to the farm, I felt a shift in the atmosphere and knew this case would be different. Upon arrival, I exited my patrol unit and immediately sensed an eerie, electric quality in the air that put me on my guard. My sixth sense was so strong it felt like fireworks going off in my gut. I conferred with the vet, who shrugged and explained what he had found. The middle-aged daughter of the elderly livestock owners barreled toward me, seething with rage and wanting to know what the hell I was going to do about their dead sheep. After calming her down, I interviewed the owners, who were extremely upset.

As I finally approached the corral, a foul and rancid stench hit me like a punch to the face. It was a strange, unnatural odor like nothing I had ever smelled before. It reeked of burning tires, burning hair, and something dead—not just the stench of rotting flesh I was expecting, having grown up working around livestock. As nausea rolled over me, I knew something was very, very wrong here. All these years later, I still remember that smell, though I never encountered it again.

The twenty-six sheep lay dead on their sides in the corral, but there were no signs of struggle around them. When livestock are attacked by wild animals like mountain lions or feral dogs, the scene is pretty much always the same: matted hair, lots of blood, entrails everywhere, and signs of panic and pandemonium in the dirt. But there was nothing like that here. Apart from the dead sheep, there was nothing amiss.

Each sheep had somehow been slit from throat to groin in a long, precise line that cut through wool and skin. Yet there was no blood. It was as if the blood had been sucked out of them, leaving not a drop behind. Their organs were intact and none of their flesh had been consumed. They were simply bloodless. The veterinarian, a man with years of experience, had never seen anything like it. He had no way to account for it. Neither did I, and when a couple of higher-ranking Rangers came out later to have a look, they were as perplexed as we were.

The sheepdogs, who normally slept with the sheep they guarded, wouldn't come near the corral. The family reported that the dogs hadn't barked once throughout the night. If an animal or person had been in the corral, the dogs would have barked, alerting the owners, and the dogs would have done their best to tear the person or predator limb from limb. The owner would certainly have heard the disturbance and come out with a gun, ready to put a bullet in whatever or whoever was messing with the sheep. But there was perfect silence, and the slaughtered sheep were only discovered in the early morning hours of the following day.

I knew from my own experience growing up around livestock that there was no human tool that could have made the cuts in the sheep's bellies. I had sheared sheep before and knew their wool was far too thick and would have had to be sheared first for someone to make a cut with such precision. Besides, the sheep would have struggled just as they do when they are being sheared, which would have made the cuts much messier. In my official opinion, no human being could have done this, especially considering the context and timeline.

The family was understandably beside themselves, angry, and terrified. The family's daughter couldn't stop yelling and blaming the world. She seemed to expect me to somehow bring all the sheep back to life. But I couldn't even explain to her what had happened to them.

Completely bewildered, I had no way to account for the sheep's demise. There simply was no plausible answer. The case remained unsolved.

But in the back of my mind, I was thinking about the skinwalker I had seen in 1986 and all the stories of UFOs I had heard over the years on the reservation. I felt certain that a paranormal element was involved here, and I wondered if there was a connection between UFOs/extraterrestrials and the dead sheep. I had heard of UFO sightings and cattle mutilations occurring together here in the Southwest and even on the reservation, but this was the first time I had encountered the phenomenon myself. Looking back now, with all my years of experience investigating cases like this one, I strongly suspect that extraterrestrials were to blame for the deaths of those sheep.

But at the time, the only thing I knew for sure was that as a Navajo Ranger, I would be dealing with far more than the traffic violations, unlawful timber harvests, and bootleggers I had encountered up to that point. Being a Navajo Ranger in the vast reaches of Navajoland would mean coming face-to-face with paranormal mysteries I wouldn't be able to explain. This unsolved case would be only the first of many.

THE THIRD WORLD

he Air-Spirit People once again gathered their belongings and left the Blue World. They wandered far and wide searching for the next world. The Wind called out to the Air-Spirit People from the South and they followed him. They found a hole in the sky. First Man created a wand of Jet, and with this the Air-Spirit People flew up to the next world.

They all passed into the Third World, the Yellow World. Bluebird had joined them, and he was the first to arrive in the Yellow World. It was a place of rivers and mountains. Holy People lived on these mountains. The Holy People were immortal and followed the path of the Rainbow and the Rays of the Sun; this is how they traveled. They were Talking God, whose body was White; Water Sprinkler, whose body was Blue; House God, whose body was Yellow; and Black God, the God of Fire. To the East lived Turquoise Boy, who was neither Male nor Female and guarded the great Male Reed; to the far West lived White Shell Girl, who was neither Female nor Male and attended to the great Female Reed, which grew along the water's edge with no tassel.

In the Fall, the Four Holy People called out to First Man and First Woman and visited them but did not speak to them. Four days in a row they visited. On the fourth day, Black God said, "You must now bathe to clean yourselves. We shall return in twelve days." First Man and First Woman carefully bathed and dried themselves with cornmeal. They listened and waited for the Holy People.

On the twelfth day the Four Holy People returned. Water Sprinkler and Black God carried a Sacred Buckskin. Talking God carried two beautiful, perfect ears of corn, completely covered with rows of perfect kernels. One ear of corn was white, the Male corn belonging to First Man. The other ear of corn was yellow in color and belonged to First Woman. The Gods placed the Sacred Buckskin upon the ground facing to the West, and the two ears of corn were placed on the Buckskin side by side with the tips pointed to the East. The feather of a White Eagle was placed under the White Ear of Corn. A Yellow Eagle feather was placed under the Yellow Ear of Corn. The People were told to stand at a distance to leave room for the Wind to do its work.

The White Wind blew upon the Sacred Buckskin. While the wind blew, the Holy People walked around the Buckskin four times as the feathers fluttered. This ceremony transformed First Man and First Woman from Air-Spirit People to that of Human Beings, with each possessing the Great Powers Human Beings now possess, to create life and children. The Holy People said, "It is here that you will live as Husband and Wife."

At the end of four days, First Woman gave birth to twins. They were neither Male nor Female. Four days later, a second set of twins were born, one Male and one Female. After twenty days, a total of five pairs of twins had been born, half Male and half Female. They were full-grown almost at once. The Holy People then took every set of twins home to the East Mountain and taught them how to properly wear the ceremonial masks and the correct way to pray. Later, they returned them to their parents.

After eight winters had passed, the twins had each found their mate among the People of the Third World, and many Human Beings were then created....

CHAPTER 3

Manhunt in the Desert
1998

I WAS ON MY BELLY, CRAWLING ON ALL FOURS THROUGH HEAVY tamarisk and Russian olive brush at the base of the San Juan River, adrenaline coursing through my veins. My team spread out ahead of me, invisible and nearly silent in the thick brush. The desert sun beat down unforgivingly on our heads, turning the damp river bottom into a humid swamp. The oil well pumps in the distance thrummed and hummed, obscuring the sounds of living things. I knew that somewhere in that brush in front of or behind me was a trio of heavily armed, cold-blooded killers who hated law enforcement and wanted me dead. My arms shook with the effort of holding up my borrowed Remington shotgun after fourteen hours in the field. As a rookie law enforcement officer, I'd been craving a chance at some real action, and now I'd discovered just what real action meant. I was filthy, hungry, exhausted, and covered in insect bites. But I was also more alive than I'd ever been before.

On May 29, 1998, I heard news that was like being shocked by a taser. Dale Claxton, an officer with the Cortez, Colorado, Police Department, had been murdered, executed in the street in broad daylight while people were driving to work and taking their children to school. He had been attempting a traffic stop on a water truck that had been stolen by members of a local militia when a man wearing camouflage stepped out of the vehicle with an assault rifle. Claxton was shot eighteen times at point-blank range, and over thirty rounds were poured into him and his patrol unit. The attack came so suddenly that he didn't have a chance to unholster his sidearm, or even take off his seat belt. At the police academy, I had been trained to prepare for the most horrific kinds of scenes, exposed to gruesome imagery and scenarios. I considered myself unflappable. But the news that an officer of the law had been murdered in such a public and vicious way cut right through all that training and preparation, hitting me straight in the heart. Besides, it was close to home, right in the Navajo Nation's backyard. It was impossible not to imagine the same thing happening to me or to my fellow Navajo Rangers.

Two other officers were seriously wounded, and seven patrol vehicles were shot up in the chase that followed Claxton's murder. The suspects fired over six hundred rounds during that early morning chase across the Colorado-Utah border, determined to keep their freedom. The fugitives, Jason Wayne McVean, Alan Lamont Pilon, and Robert "Bobby" Mason, abandoned the water truck, stole another vehicle, and finally took off into the Utah desert on foot. It was a desolate area with very few trees, filled with red rock canyons—a desert theater as cinematic as any movie set. A week later, Mason had another gunfight with authorities near the Swinging Bridge that crosses the San Juan River, injuring a sheriff's deputy in the process. Cornered and unwilling to surrender himself to police, Mason committed suicide in a makeshift bunker filled with pipe bombs, leaving only McVean and Pilon at large.

A monthslong manhunt ensued, with hundreds of officers deployed to capture the men who had murdered Dale Claxton. These vicious criminals belonged to one of several militias that were active in the region at that time. These anti-government paramilitary groups trained with firearms and explosives, using information and techniques from military training manuals. They were highly organized with designated leaders, regular meetings, and uniforms that included military fatigues, patches, and emblems. They were likely planning to turn that stolen water truck into a bomb, possibly to blow up the dam at Lake Powell.

In the years leading up to 2000, in the midst of the Y2K craze that swept the nation, people feared a massive electronic crash that would herald financial collapse, planes falling from the sky, and generally the end of the world. Militia groups like the one that killed Claxton had spent years prepping for this moment—storing supplies and training themselves for the apocalypse, eager for societal collapse. They were numerous in the surrounding areas, and officers had been warned to avoid them while alone on patrol. Some commanders wouldn't let their officers patrol certain backcountry areas at all because militia were known to be training there. They were dangerous, armed to the teeth, and full of nothing but hatred for law enforcement and government.

This is who Dale Claxton encountered on that fateful morning, and this is who I—a rookie Navajo Ranger not even finished with field training—was determined to help bring to justice. I hadn't expected to be involved in a SWAT mission so early in my career, but when the opportunity presented itself, there was no way I could turn it down. This is what I'd dreamed of as a little boy and imagined as I went through the grueling training at the police academy—to go after the bad guys and make them pay.

My sergeant at the time, Elmer Phillips, asked me if I would be willing to assist the Shiprock Police with the Four Corners Manhunt. He said a Navajo Police lieutenant, Clarence Hawthorne, needed a way to haul the department's watercraft up to the Montezuma Creek, Utah, area on the San Juan River. They would use the canoes to conduct water operations and monitoring. I agreed and drove the canoes an hour and a half from Window Rock to Four Corners. I arrived at a school in Montezuma Creek, where the Incident Command was located, a place swarming with law enforcement officers in tactical gear and camouflage. There were local police, various law enforcement officers from surrounding areas, National Guard members, and FBI. A bit awestruck by the spectacle, I turned my keys over to a Navajo Police officer, who left to take the canoes to where they would be staged.

While I waited, I was hanging out with some of the officers on the Navajo Police Strategic Response Team, or SRT, some of whom I knew and had worked with before. They asked if I wanted to go out on a mission with one of the SRTs. Maybe I ought to have been afraid, but my training had prepared me for the dangerous nature of law enforcement, and Claxton's death had certainly driven the point home. To hold the kind of job I did meant trusting my life to the Creator's hands. It wasn't in my nature to turn down a chance to jump in and get involved; I was nearly always the first to volunteer whenever there was a need. Plus, with an opportunity this exciting, there was no way I could say no. I didn't have any tactical gear with me, but Lieutenant Hawthorne said that he had a Remington 12-gauge shotgun I could use. Another guy loaned me a woodland camo BDU, or Battle Dress Uniform, shirt. I got a quick lesson in the art of camouflaging my face with camo paint and a crash course in tactics and a tactical glossary.

My assignment was "Tail-end Charlie." This position was the last member at the back of a SWAT team stack, and it was my job to protect the team from behind and not let anyone sneak up on them. This is how I found myself belly down in the river bottom, hotter and itchier than I'd ever been in my life, my arms exhausted from holding up that Remington shotgun.

But I was exhilarated. I remembered how I'd watched the hubbub and excitement of the manhunt in the Oklahoma Girl Scout Murders as a little boy, and now I was part of one myself. The helicopters, armored tactical units, and SWAT operations thrilled me. I couldn't believe that they had trusted me enough to invite me to participate in such an important operation. I wasn't afraid for my own life. I only cared about finding the men we sought. Even so early on in my career, I had already become part of the brotherhood of law enforcement, and I took Claxton's brutal murder personally, like a slap in the face to all law enforcement. It was a challenge from the militia, and we were determined to meet it head-on.

We worked together to search the areas along the San Juan River, looking particularly in the areas under the bank of the river that militiamen had cleared out to store supplies and provide hiding places. This area was a spiderweb of red rock canyons, which made it difficult to search systematically, especially since the fugitives knew the terrain better than we did. Thus, in addition to the men on the ground, there were helicopters with forward-looking infrared in the air and bloodhounds searching for the faintest scent of our quarry.

The weather was extremely hot during the daytime—with the humidity, it felt like 110 degrees—and at night the temperatures would drop. The sweltering heat was nearly unbearable, and some outsiders who weren't used to the climate actually passed out. Once, the sun let up for a moment and rain began to sprinkle from the sky, providing welcome relief. But it was only a trick because after about thirty minutes of coolness, the river bottom turned into a steaming cauldron of hell, so hot and humid we wished to have the miserable desert sun back again. The rain only made the sand stick to us and our clothes, and once the sand got in your clothes, you were screwed. The previously soft fabric of your clothing became like sandpaper, resulting in the areas around your neck, armpits, waist, and ankles being literally sanded raw.

Insects swarmed us, and by the end of the day I had about three hundred insect bites from about seven different types of insects—mosquitoes, gnats, flies, and God only knows what else. We wore boonie hats like those used in the Vietnam War, with mosquito nets that covered our faces. We bathed in military grade insect repellent and covered our skin with mud, but nothing helped. By the time I made it home, I looked like I'd survived a plague.

Despite the extreme discomfort, I couldn't risk scratching myself. Any stray movements could put me and my entire team in danger, so I watched the mosquitoes grow fat with my blood, unable to do anything about it. I had to draw on my training from the Indian Police Academy, those days of doing push-ups in a field of thorns or on burning blacktop. I had to control my emotions and reactions to physical sensations, focusing solely on our objective. The physical discomfort was something to overcome through sheer force of will, pushing the itching, burning, and exhaustion I felt to the back of my mind and bringing all my senses to bear on the fugitives who were creeping through this same terrain, as intent on eluding capture as we were on capturing them.

To this day, I can still remember the sounds and smells of the river and the oil fields like it was yesterday, hearing the constant drum of the pumpjacks—some near, some far away. This sound aided the killers as sound camouflage, masking their every movement. Also masking their movement were the livestock and wildlife, like deer and beaver, along the river bottom. With my nerves taut as trip wires and my reflexes on overdrive, there were numerous times that I almost shot either a cow or horse moving through the brush.

Despite the misery and stress of these conditions, I stayed for a few days going on several missions in the bush, each day learning more and more about SWAT tactics. How to track. How to improvise, be flexible, and deal with anything that came up. How to pay attention and control my emotions so that I could stay alive and avoid getting anyone else on my team killed. It was exhilarating, and I drank up every single moment. I loved the tactical operations, specialized weapons and equipment, and intense atmosphere of SWAT. The experience would soon after inspire me to become a federal firearms instructor. I had always loved shooting and had been used to handling guns since childhood, but being involved in the manhunt made me want to take that interest and do something practical and essential with my knowledge and appreciation of firearms.

I finally had to leave the field when my clothes were so grungy they could've stood up by themselves. I went home for a shower and some clean clothes, to get a good night's sleep, and the most critical thing: to pick up my carbine rifle. I was sick to death of lugging that old Remington shotgun through the desert.

I arrived back at Montezuma Creek refreshed and better equipped to be out on tactical missions. When I returned, I was briefed on the latest intel and was assigned to what was called an Observation Point, or OP. I couldn't believe it. I was extremely excited about being accepted as an SRT or SWAT team member, which was a feat unto itself. I had images in my head of tactical officers hanging off the end of a rappelling rope or fast-roping from a helicopter, or a Navy Seal slowly emerging from out of the water, face painted in camouflage, dressed in a black BDU and wielding a machine gun. But I didn't let on about my excitement; I just played it off, nonchalantly saying, "That's cool." Inside, though, I was prouder than I had ever been before.

Making things even more exciting, the OP was a night op. I was assigned with Navajo Police officer Cornelius Thomas, better known as Corny. After introductions, he and I hit it off and he gave me instructions in the use and functions of the night vision goggles, or NVGs, we'd be using that night. He went over the weapon system that was assigned to him, a scoped bolt-action Remington 700 rifle. I cleaned and lubed my Colt carbine one last time. As the time passed, the sun's light slowly started to fade. I grew more and more excited as darkness set in, adrenaline pumping and my senses on overload. We went over the maps and our gear, making sure we had everything with us. We loaded our equipment into Corny's patrol unit and set out into uncharted territory.

He had driven quite a distance in the dark, all without headlights. When we got to our designated point, he pulled the unit off the worn, sandy ruts of the road and turned the ignition off. We tried to tune in to our senses: seeing, hearing, smelling—and the most important of all, the mysterious sixth sense I had been learning to hone as a rookie Navajo Ranger. We sat in the patrol unit with the windows rolled down for quite a while, listening and assessing each little noise, to determine if that particular sound was natural to the area or something that was out of the ordinary and didn't belong. However, the incessant drone of the oil pumps made that nearly impossible. The smells of the desert filled the vehicle: sage, oil from the wool of the goats and sheep that have grazed this same range over the decades, and the pungent petroleum from the oil fields.

We were located at the edge of a sheer sandstone cliff on the south side of the San Juan River. After we unloaded all of our equipment, Corny settled on a cot to rest, and I took first watch, moving twenty or thirty feet away. Initially, I grabbed standard binoculars, but only a very few sources of light could be seen. There were some car headlights and taillights and lights on some of the oil wells, but the rest was a vast black void. Then I picked up the night vision goggles, turned the power on, and put the optics up to my eyes. I was amazed at what came into view. Everything took on a green hue, but details that were not there previously began to appear—the trees and sagebrush and the river far below. As I continued scanning around, I looked toward the sky and was blown away. I was able to see what had to be millions and millions of stars that are simply not visible with the naked eye. I scanned out across the valley, which was bathed in a green light. I was amazed at how any existing light was greatly amplified, even from very far away. It was my first time using military-grade night vision goggles, and I felt like a kid with a new toy, almost giddy.

I continued to watch over the pitch-black river valley below, but when there was nothing to see, I would return to stargazing. As I watched, I began following what I initially thought was a satellite, but all of a sudden it veered off its trajectory, startling me. Then it began moving and turning back on itself and circling around, kind of like a bumblebee in a field of flowers. Whatever the craft or object was, its movement was incredible. It did not have any engine noise or emit any other sounds. I put the NVGs aside, and after I regained my usual nighttime eyesight, I could still see the object, which was amber in color. I was tempted to holler at Corny, but I figured by the time I got over to him the object would be gone. Sure enough, within a minute or so, as I was watching it, the object simply vanished and was gone.

Many years later, in 2008, I would see it again. The northern part of the reservation had seen a series of severe storms with heavy rainfall, so the water level was very high on the San Juan River. Lieutenant Jon Dover and I were informed that a person had drowned while attempting to swim across the river somewhere near Copper Canyon. Previous attempts to recover the body had been unsuccessful, so Jon and I put the department's seventeen-foot Lowe patrol boat in the water at Lake Powell near Page, Arizona, to assist with trying to locate the body. We worked our way westward, fighting the white-capped waves. We had gotten many miles up the San Juan, but then suddenly we ran into a heavy debris field of logs and branches and did not want to risk damaging the propeller, so we chose to pull the boat ashore and camp for the night as it was getting late.

We set up camp and ate. While I was lying on my cot, my belly full of pork and beans and an MRE, or Meal Ready to Eat, the sky grew dark. As I was admiring the beauty of the stars, suddenly I observed an amber-colored light or orb that appeared about two or three times larger than the average satellite. But unlike a satellite, this object was moving in a clear and consistent, sharp zigzag pattern. As I watched it, I hollered over to my partner, "Hey, Jon, what is that?"

I pointed at the object, which he then began watching. The object was moving across the sky from the west to the east. As it approached the 12 o'clock position, we could clearly see two F-16 military fighter jets with their afterburners on following directly behind the object. When the object had moved just a little past the 12 o'clock position, it instantly accelerated toward the east while maintaining the same zigzag pattern. It was all the way on the edge of the eastern horizon in less than two seconds. The object had left the two F-16s sitting practically still. The speed and performance of the object was certainly not of this world. I had never witnessed anything move at such a speed, ever. Given the distance the object covered and the time, it would have to have been traveling something like ten thousand miles per hour. The otherworldly speed at which the object traveled was simply beyond belief.

But what really surprised me was how familiar it was: The size and color of this object exactly matched the object I had seen many, many years earlier while I was standing on a sheer sandstone cliff, a rookie Navajo Ranger on his first SWAT mission, on the Four Corners Manhunt. Once more I could smell the oil derricks and sage and feel the excitement and wonder of a young man facing the vast, unknowable reaches of the universe.

That night in Four Corners, seeing something unexplainable through a pair of night vision goggles, reawakened the childlike curiosity about UFOs I had as a little boy, and to this day, I remain deeply interested in and inspired by the search for extraterrestrial life. But, of course, that night in the midst of a manhunt, my mind was too much on our fugitives to think long of UFOs. There were things much closer to earth I needed to worry about. I turned my attention away from the otherworldly lights of heaven and looked straight down below the cliff's edge, where I caught sight of something unexpected, this time much closer at hand. My heart skipped a beat.

"Holy shit! What is that?" I muttered to myself.

There was a bright square object just below us. This square was located on the north side of the river. As I watched, I couldn't believe what I was seeing. I then took the NVGs away and tried to view the object with my own eyes. I thought maybe I was just seeing things because the square disappeared. Then I looked with the NVGs again, and sure enough there was the square. I knew this area had been repeatedly cleared several times and was supposed to be secure. So, there should not have been anyone or anything down there along the water's edge.

I continued to watch the square for about five or ten minutes. As I observed, I was able to detect movement around this object. I tried to imagine what could create what I was seeing. Then it occurred to me, what if someone had built a small fire in a pit underground, and then used something like a tarp or board to cover it? That would cause light coming out around the edge of the tarp, creating the image I was seeing. I took off over to where Corny was resting his eyes.

"Hey, Corny, I think I spotted something," I said nervously, trying to keep the excitement from my voice.

He was probably thinking to himself, *Geez . . . rookies!* But he gradually got up from his comfortable cot and followed me back to my previous position.

"What is it?" he asked, annoyed.

I handed him the NVGs and said, "Look right down there!" I grabbed his arm and pointed it at the location.

He took one look through the goggles and replied, just as I had, "Holy shit!"

I was laughing to myself, thinking, *See, I told you so!* But, of course, I knew better than to run my mouth.

"What is it though?" he muttered.

I said, "To me, it looks as though someone built a fire underground, in a pit. Then they've got it covered with something to try and prevent you from seeing the light, but with the NVGs it amplifies the light so much you can see its glow. If you try to see this thing with just the naked eye you can't see any light at all." I hesitated. "Plus, if you look close you can actually see two people moving in and around that light."

Corny's head swiveled toward me, and he grinned. "Damn, Milford, I think you might have actually found something!"

We continued to observe some more, but within about five more minutes, he radioed our SRT contact on the north side of the river. He used code to say that we had possibly spotted the suspects. We kept watching the light and the movement around the object, but in about twenty minutes the light went out and never came back on. Other team members arrived at our location, but we were unable to show them anything as the light had disappeared.

The ground team was working their way to the location we had given them. When we started to get some light just before sunrise, we were able to use binocs and the scope on the Remington 700 rifle to glass the area where we had observed the activity. Sure enough, we could see a spot not too far from the water's edge where the sand had a lot of fresh human footprints. There had been someone at the location only an hour earlier!

As a young man fresh out of the police academy, excited for my first real action, this was extremely frustrating and disappointing. It seemed as though we had almost had them. We were so damn close, but no cigar . . . at least not this time. I kept thinking about an old saying I'd often heard: "'Almost' only counts in horseshoes and hand grenades."

This cat-and-mouse situation continued for months, with occasional sightings of the fugitives that yielded no results. Undeterred, we continued operations and conducted numerous missions into the river bottom and up into the higher red rock formations overlooking the whole valley and canyon. I didn't have a close-up encounter with the fugitives during that manhunt. But I did experience something far, far stranger.

I had been out in the field with Lieutenant Hawthorne's tactical operation team, or TOT. We spent the day hiking, climbing, and clearing various canyons and arroyos in the extreme heat. In the evening, we finally made our way back to the base camp at the Montezuma Creek school. By the time we arrived, it had started to get dark. Someone hollered for me to see some of the staff who had chow waiting for us. I first went to put away some of my gear and wash my face and hands as I was completely covered in dirt, sweat, grit, and general filth, my eyes bleary from debris and fatigue. Once I could actually see again, I headed over to get something to eat, now completely starving. When I got to where the food was set up, I found I was the last guy in. There were a couple of cardboard boxes on the tailgate of a pickup truck. I went over and peeked in one. There in one corner of the box was a stale piece of frybread that was so hard it could have been used as an edged weapon.

At that point, I was afraid to look over into the other box. But I finally gathered my courage and discovered it held several empty plastic bags that had once contained loaves of sliced bread; now there was nothing but crumbs to be found. There were also a few pieces of wilted lettuce, a couple of tomatoes that appeared to have been run over by a truck, and a partial slice of bologna. I took the stale frybread and piece of bologna and limped back toward my unit. At least I did get *something* to eat that night. In reality, I think I was too tired and beat to care. I did realize that I was being watched from afar and probably provided some comic relief for some lucky individuals. I learned a valuable lesson that night, though: If you planned on eating anything while on this operation, you better act like a stray rez mutt and fight your way to the front of the line as soon as you got back, and any washing up could be done later. This was not the time or place for good manners.

Once I got back to my patrol unit and choked down my dinner, I then pulled my bedroll from the toolbox on my truck bed and placed it underneath the flatbed trailer that was still attached to the hitch on my unit. I sat on the edge of the trailer and worked on prying off my boots that were basically welded to my feet. I then climbed underneath the trailer and lay facedown, thoroughly exhausted, and pulled a military type of netting over my head and face to keep the critters off.

As drowsiness took over, I tried to reposition myself into a more comfortable position and turned my head to the right. Through squinted eyes I glimpsed someone or something lying right next to me. Startled, I flinched and jerked backward away from this thing and hit my head on the underside of the trailer. Something had been right next to me, just inches away. It appeared to be a black mass in the shape of a human being, but in an instant, whatever had been there vanished. I had experienced sleep paralysis before, but I knew that this wasn't that. It was entirely real, not a trick of my tired mind. I could have reached out and touched the entity if I had chosen to.

But I was too exhausted to be afraid—or to feel much of anything except the desperate desire to sleep undisturbed. I crawled out from under the trailer and grabbed my sleeping bag and threw it in the bed of my truck, where I slept for the remainder of the night, with my carbine rifle lying next to me.

What I witnessed that night did have a humanlike form, but its outline did not have clearly defined edges. It was shadowy and almost like smoke, but I could not see completely through it. Even though I didn't identify any eyes or distinct facial features, I did sense this thing's head was turned toward me and was looking right at me. It reminded me strongly of my encounter with the skinwalker, that feeling of being watched with menace and malice. I don't know if this was a past human spirit, a demonic entity, or something related to witchcraft.

Perhaps, while I was hunting those fugitives, something else was hunting me.

After that experience, I watched out not only for the militiamen, but also for whatever desert entity had found me in the vulnerable moments before I fell asleep.

The manhunt gradually started to wind down a couple of weeks later, and sightings of the fugitives grew further and further apart. One afternoon we received word that the teams would be standing down. Despite my excitement at being part of a manhunt, this was music to my ears. I was exhausted after weeks of operations in the desert heat and constant, unrelenting vigilance.

One of the Navajo Police Department's commanding officers, Tyrone Benally, was in charge of much of the logistics. I ran into him as I was getting my gear together. He said, "Stan, you look like you could use a good night's rest."

I laughed. "Yeah, I'm pretty burnt."

He told me there was a room available up the road at the Super 8 in Blanding if I wanted to use it before my long drive home.

I said, "Hell yeah! Thanks!" So, I piled all my belongings into my patrol unit and headed north to Blanding.

I got to the motel, where there was no parking—the whole place was crawling with law enforcement. I registered, then went to my room and took a seriously long, hot shower to wash many days of crud off. Once I got out, I felt like a new man. I walked just north of the motel to a steak house and ordered the biggest, medium-rare, prime rib steak on the menu, with all the fixin's: Caesar salad, baked potato, green beans, garlic toast, and a tall iced tea to wash it down.

Food had never tasted so good, and I ate until I was about to burst. Full and satisfied for the first time in weeks, I went back to the room and piled up in bed watching cable TV. The last thing I remember was watching the news, and they were talking about the manhunt I'd just participated in. Seeing it on TV was slightly surreal, my first experience of viewing the part I played in an operation from someone else's eyes. Though my role in the manhunt felt like everything to me, I was only one small part of a much larger enterprise. And now my part was over.

I fell into a deep sleep, not worrying about fugitives or creepy desert entities. There was only the simple comfort of a cozy bed and a chance to finally get some real rest.

The next thing I knew, the telephone was ringing. I woke, the lamp on the nightstand still on and the TV still murmuring in the background. It took me a second to figure out where the hell I was. Then I leaned over and picked up the phone.

"Hello?" I croaked.

"Hello? Is this Ranger Milford?" a woman asked.

"Yeah," I said, still groggy and disoriented.

"This is the Shiprock dispatcher with the Navajo Police. Milford, I think we have those fugitives sighted at a residence, south toward Montezuma Creek. We can't get ahold of any of the Navajo Police officers up there. Can you see if you can get ahold of anyone and respond?"

I said, "Yeah, I'll let them know."

I hung up and then went and looked out the window into the dark, shocked to discover that the parking lot that just a few hours earlier was completely full of patrol units from numerous law enforcement agencies was now empty, except for a few civilian vehicles. I did manage to spot one Navajo Police unit. I yanked on my BDU pants and ran down to the motel's front desk. I told them who I was and that I needed to contact the Navajo Police officers who were still there, that it was an emergency.

They rang the room and gave me the room number, and I sprinted down the hall. The door eased open at my knock. Breathlessly, I explained what was going on. The senior Navajo Police officer asked if I had any tactical equipment.

"Yeah!" I said. My adrenaline was already flowing once more, my thoughts torn between the excitement of potentially catching the fugitives and the possibility that going after them could mean my own demise.

"Get your gear on and meet us at the patrol unit," the officer said.

Heart racing, I geared up and met them in the parking lot with my carbine rifle and my backpack. I threw my stuff in the backseat and we were off, heading south toward Montezuma Creek. From the back seat of the Chevrolet Caprice, I watched with wide eyes as the blue digital glow of the speedometer climbed to one hundred and fifteen. After that I stopped looking, not even wanting to know just how fast we were going. We kept the sirens off, of course, needing the element of surprise, and only turned the police lights on occasionally to alert oncoming vehicles. We rocketed through the dark desert night, eager and ready for action.

At that speed, most of the trip felt like we were airborne. When we'd hit these little hills, it felt like the tires actually left contact with the blacktop. Within a few minutes, we were almost to Montezuma Creek. Soon, we turned off on a small dirt road to the east. According to the dispatcher, an elderly Navajo man had been visiting his son's house late that night, which was about a mile away from his home. She said that when the son got ready to take the elderly man home, they could see a flashlight shining near his house. They then called the Navajo Police dispatcher. They moved closer toward the house, but the flashlight went out. They said they could hear two people climbing on the rocks of the mesa behind the house. They said whoever it was would fall or trip every now and then and would be cursing—and the voices belonged to young Anglo or non-Navajo individuals.

Once we got to the scene, I was assigned to secure the front part of the house. The two Navajo Police officers were going to try and track the fugitives who had been outside the house on the mesa. I was told to use whatever force was necessary to stop anyone who came out of the house, as the house had not been cleared. I was hyped-up on adrenaline and ready for anything, including a shoot-out if it came to that. I was a confident marksman, more than ready to test my skills if I needed to. But no one ever came out.

Soon, a few Cortez sheriff's deputies arrived on scene. I briefed them with the information I had. They went into the house and cleared it as the sun began to rise. Before long, several Navajo Police officers and criminal investigators also arrived at the location. When the two Navajo Police officers I had come with got back to the house, we all debriefed. The law enforcement officers who had since arrived took over. The two Navajo Police officers and I left to return to Blanding. We got back to the motel, and I loaded my patrol unit and left for home, disappointed again. We were right on their tail, but we just couldn't catch them. Even so, I'm very patient by nature, so I thought to myself, *You guys got away this time, but you won't always.*

But in the coming months it seemed as though the fugitives had turned into ghosts and slipped away into thin air—no arrests, no sightings, no nothing. I could not grasp how these guys had managed to slip through the fingers of some five hundred law enforcement officers. But then again, they were militia. They had trained and planned, and trained and planned some more, just like law enforcement does. They had all the time in the world to plan for this event, and they knew the terrain well; one of them had practically grown up in the oil fields.

Still, I felt certain that we would locate them eventually. I continued to take "the scenic tour" through Montezuma Creek every weekend when I was either going home to Sawmill, Arizona, or was going back to my regular patrol in Monument Valley, in the chance that I might get lucky—or unlucky as the case may be—and come across these guys.

About a month later, I did have a strange incident while patrolling west on the highway near the Four Corners region. I had just passed the turnoff to the north that goes to Hovenweep. All of a sudden, there was a white, older-model pickup truck approaching in the opposite lane of traffic. As it passed, a red flag immediately went up in my mind, though it took me a few moments to realize why. The vehicle had a Tommy Gate, which is an aftermarket hydraulic lift that replaces the existing tailgate. The vehicle appeared to be an oil field maintenance utility truck, like what is used in the oil fields in the area. The thing that did not fit was the two occupants had black faces, but the hands on the steering wheel were white. Their faces were painted black!

It took a couple of seconds to register. I thought to myself, *What the hell? Did I just see what I thought I did?* I looked in my rearview mirror only to see that the passenger was sitting up in his seat looking back through the rear window, watching me. I then lost sight of the vehicle as it went over the crest of a hill.

Heart thumping so hard I could hear and feel my pulse in my ears, I did a U-turn to follow the truck. I tried to radio Shiprock Police, but I was unable to get through because of the distance from the dispatch and the rocky terrain obstructing the signal. I knew that I needed to keep a little space between me and the truck in case it was the fugitives. They would certainly have no compunction about shooting me dead, just as they had Dale Claxton. As I got up near the Hovenweep turnoff, I witnessed the dust trail and vehicle going north on the Hovenweep road. I turned off and followed the truck. Again, I tried to radio the Shiprock Police, to no avail. This wasn't a surprise, as communication in such a remote region was always patchy and unreliable; besides, backup was likely an hour and a half away anyway.

When I got to the top of the hill, I was shocked at what I saw. The vehicle was down below and had nearly crossed the entire valley. The driver had to be doing nearly a hundred miles an hour on this uneven dirt road. Again, I tried to contact any local law enforcement without success. I continued to follow at a manageable speed, and I kept my carbine rifle close. I figured I might find the vehicle crashed somewhere along the road considering its extreme speed. But I didn't; instead, the vehicle had vanished. I never heard that a similar truck had been stolen or that these individuals had any other run-ins with police, but I have always wondered if they were part of the militia that killed Claxton, or perhaps even the very fugitives we sought.

Some months later, I was talking to two retired pilots visiting the Antelope Canyon viewpoint, south of Page, Arizona, and Lake Powell. They said that about a month before the killing of officer Dale Claxton, they were in an area called Jackass Canyon near Hovenweep. They said they had pulled up into a little cove that looked like a good place to set up camp. They got out and began unloading all their camping supplies from the shell camper on the back of their truck, when all of a sudden someone behind them opened fire with a fully automatic machine gun. They ducked in terror; then, out walks this heavyset guy covered in camouflage from head to toe, packing an AK-47 machine gun. He strode up to them and asked what they were doing. They replied that they were going to camp out for a few days.

He told them, "No, you're not! At least not here, you're not. Me and a few of my friends are doing tactical maneuvers here this weekend. You guys need to leave."

The visitors grabbed their belongings and tore out of there in a cloud of dust.

They told me they were 100 percent sure this guy was one of the three fugitives who killed Dale Claxton, identifying him as Alan Lamont Pilon. They recognized him from the FBI wanted posters and from the newspapers. They said from his strange behavior and because his pupils were completely dilated, he appeared to be under the influence of drugs. I felt these two individuals were lucky to have escaped from Pilon unharmed. I only wished that he could have been apprehended after this encounter, before Claxton's death and all that ensued.

In the end, there was no grand shoot-out between the outlaws and law enforcement like on *Starsky & Hutch,* nor was there a hostage situation or anything else that looks exciting on TV. Instead, time passed: hours, days, weeks, months, and then years. The memories of those days gradually faded into the dusty, high-desert sunset.

In October of 1999, Pilon's remains were discovered by hunters in Squaw Canyon, along with a tent, backpack, and gun. Pilon's ankle was broken, and he had a gunshot wound to the head. It was unclear whether the gunshot wound was self-inflicted or not. McVean was still at large and remained so for several more years.

Then, in June of 2007, a sixty-one-year-old cowboy named Eric Bayles was riding horseback following a hundred head of cattle when he came across a small piece of fabric and a metal bar half buried in the desert trail. Bayles climbed down off his horse and cleared some of the soil away from the object. As he scooped the soil with his hands, he could see it was the frame of a backpack. As he pulled it from the ground, he unearthed the remaining nylon pack. Inside were bullets, gun magazines, a camouflage flak vest, and pipe bombs. Close by were an AK-47 machine gun and Jason McVean's bones and the remains of his bullet-shattered skull.

This cowboy's chance discovery lying in the dirt marked the end of what was known as the Four Corners Manhunt.

We may not have caught the men we sought on that manhunt, which was disappointing to me as a young man with a thirst for justice. But I did learn an immense amount about SWAT, as well as law enforcement more generally. Most important, I developed my sixth sense, that gut instinct that would stay with me for the rest of my career. Later, as I got into investigating paranormal cases, I assimilated that ability, learning to pick up not only on material threats but also on negative, harmful energies. In the same way I learned to control my emotions and keep myself safe from human assailants, I would learn to identify whether paranormal entities were benign or wished me harm.

Of course, I didn't know it then, but that heightened state of urgency I entered while on the Four Corners Manhunt—that mindset of extreme vigilance, every sense taut and ready for the worst that could happen— was exactly the state of mind I would need once I became The Paranormal Ranger. From SWAT operations, I learned to prepare as well as I could beforehand and then listen to my sixth sense, that gut instinct that told me where to go and where not to go, when to stay still and when to move quickly. This ability to trust my instincts would serve me for the rest of my career. I learned to be ready for the unexpected before I even walked out of my front door, to prepare myself for the worst that could happen on the job and to know exactly how I would respond when it did.

I never imagined that what was on the other side of my front door might be paranormal in nature, but perhaps I should have. Despite my lack of interest in going looking for the paranormal, the paranormal certainly seemed determined to come looking for me. Skinwalkers, ghosts, UFOs, and other entities had so far been unavoidable in my life, so when they became a part of my career, perhaps I shouldn't have been surprised.

THE ORIGIN OF MONSTERS

In the Third World, First Man was a proficient hunter. One day he came home, bearing a big deer that he had hunted and killed, and delivered it proudly to his wife, First Woman. First Woman accepted his offering, then looked down at her lap and said, "Thank you, my Womanhood, for bringing this deer." First Man was confused and asked First Woman what she meant by this. First Woman said, "I meant that you brought this fine deer because you want to lie with me, but Women could easily live without Men. Women are the ones who gather the wild plants and tend to our gardens. We don't really need Men to help us survive. Therefore, I thank my Womanhood."

Her words enraged First Man, who left their home and called a meeting with all the other Men. He told them how First Woman had insulted the contributions of Men. They too were offended and grew angry. Collectively the men said, "If Women think they can live without us Men, let them try."

The First Man and the other Men, along with the twins who were neither Male nor Female, set out to cross the river to live on the other side. They carried all their tools they had created, such as axes and hoes. They carried baskets, bowls, and grinding stones the twins had made too, leaving none of these for the Women's use. As they tried to cross the river, the powerful current pulled many of them under the water, drowning them.

The Women suffered too. As the years passed, they produced less and less food simply because they had no tools to tend to the garden. The Men were able to produce plenty of food, but they missed the company of the Women more and more. The Women and Men desired and longed for each other's company and found no joy or happiness in living without their mates.

There was a time of terrible transgression, when Women and Men, desperate for each other's touch, pleasured themselves with various objects. Finally, the Owl called out to the Men and Women and said, "The manner in which you are living is wrong and must immediately stop. No good will ever come of this separation." He was right, as they would soon learn. From this time of transgression, many terrible Monsters would be born.

Heeding the Owl's advice, First Man called to First Woman across the river and said, "First Woman, do you still think you can live without Man?" First Woman called out to First Man, "No, I do not think I can live without Man." First Man apologized for his behavior toward First Woman. "I am very sorry I let the things you said make me angry."

The Owl said, "Men and Women shall return to each other and once again live as Husband and Wife and will never live apart." Then a raft was sent across the river and brought the Women over to the Men's side. Then Man and Woman bathed and dried their bodies with dried cornmeal, but they remained apart for that night in repentance. The following day Man and Woman returned to their proper life together, never to separate again.

When Man and Woman came back together, a Mother and Two Daughters had been in the fields and had not seen the raft. They were left behind on the Women's side of the river. They decided to swim across. As they did, Big Water Creature grabbed the Two Daughters and dragged them to her home under the water. For three days the Two Daughters could not be found.

On the morning of the fourth day, Talking God and Water Sprinkler appeared with two large bowls. One bowl was filled with White Shell, and the other was filled with Blue Shell. They placed the bowls at the water's edge. Talking God and Water Sprinkler began to spin the bowls. The spinning bowls created a whirlpool in the water that opened and led down to Big Water Creature's house. First Man and First Woman traveled down the passage and into the home, followed by Coyote First Angry. They found Big Water Creature asleep in a chair. They found Big Water Creature's Two Children, along with the missing Two Daughters. First Man and First Woman grabbed the hands of the two girls, and Coyote First Angry hid Big Water Creature's Two Children in his fur-lined skin coat. First Man and First Woman led the Two Daughters through the passage back to the safety of the bank. That night the People held a great celebration for the return of the Two Daughters.

The next morning, many animals ran in terror past the People's Village from the East, and their stampede continued for three days. On the fourth day, the People sent the Insect Scouts called Locust and White Locust to the East to see what had frightened the animals. The Locusts quickly returned with the news that a flood was coming toward the Village from three different directions. The People climbed to the top of Sisnaajiní Mountain. First Man ran to each of the Sacred Mountains; he grasped dirt in his hands from each Mountain before joining the others on top of Sisnaajiní Mountain. Turquoise Boy came bearing the great Male Reed. First Man planted the reed on top of the mountain. The people blew wind, and the reed grew and grew until it reached the Sky. Woodpecker hollowed out the reed to make a passage for the People to travel. The People, Four Holy People, and Turquoise Boy began to climb up the reed until they reached the Fourth World, the waters of the flood surging at their feet....

CHAPTER 4

The Paranormal Rangers
2000

THINGS DIDN'T SLOW DOWN FOR ME AFTER THE FOUR CORNERS Manhunt. So far, my career as a Navajo Ranger had meant jumping headfirst into dangerous and exciting work, and that's how it continued to be. Only a few years out of the police academy, I was moved from Monument Valley to Window Rock, where I was put in charge of a Special Projects Unit that handled special, high-profile, and sensitive cases, such as dignitary protection detail, event security, tactical operations, special events, and anything important that fell outside the usual duties of a Navajo Ranger. My partner, Lieutenant Jonathan Dover, and I worked these cases together, often developing protocols from scratch and putting plans together as a team.

We quickly proved to the newly instated Chief Navajo Ranger, Leonard Butler, whom I'd met during the Four Corners Manhunt when he was the Navajo Police Chief, that we could handle anything he assigned to us; he knew he could trust our knowledge, problem-solving, and steadiness, so he came to rely on us more and more. We provided dignitary protection at the Navajo Nation Fair for the first woman to run for president on the Navajo Reservation; coordinated security at the 2002 Winter Olympics, at which the Navajo Nation had a large presence; and were co-SWAT team commanders for backcountry operations. These operations included ones like Operation Black Flag, during which we conducted reconnaissance in remote areas to search for items affiliated with the production of crystal methamphetamine.

Jon Dover and I had known each other for years, from back in my days as a rookie recruit—he was already an experienced ranger when I was doing livestock inspections. One of the names that popped up repeatedly was Jonathan Dover. Back then—and even still today—he was someone to look up to. All of the Navajo Rangers had a presence about them, but when I had dreamed of becoming a ranger too, it was Jon who I had in mind. He was a clean-cut, sturdy man who radiated wisdom and authority. He seemed so *together*—his uniform was always pressed and neat, his manners were professional, and his confidence and skill as a ranger were obvious. In my eyes, Jon was the exemplary ranger—a prototype ranger. He was knowledgeable in all areas of law enforcement and natural resource enforcement, everything from public safety to forestry, fish and game, agriculture, and livestock. He was well-read and seemed to always have the answers to everything; he was a veritable encyclopedia on all things related to law enforcement.

He was also completely fearless, which enabled him to perform well at SWAT operations because he was able to implement and rely on what he was trained to do and focus on the mission at hand and not be distracted by fear. His knowledge and understanding of SWAT tactics and procedures, plus having good sound judgment and common sense, allowed him to excel as a team commander. Most Navajos are terrified of snakes, but I've seen Jon catch and remove one without even flinching. He credits his fearlessness to his strong traditional Navajo faith and spirituality. He uses his knowledge of traditional teachings in prayer and personal protection rituals. Jon is respectful of medicine men and traditional practitioners and practices many of their teachings.

In short, for me as a rookie ranger, Jon, who was ten years my senior, was a person well worth knowing, so I always jumped at a chance to work with him, like when he asked me to help with security at a livestock auction during my first year as a ranger. I was very happy when we were made partners, and that attitude never changed over many years of working together. In the beginning of our relationship, Jon was a mentor—someone to learn from and emulate—but over the years he became more like a brother. The more I got to know him, the more I found to respect and admire, but he always treated me like an equal.

We also had a great deal in common. We had both been raised in two worlds—mainstream Western culture and Native American culture. Jon is part Navajo, Filipino, and Apache Tribe of Oklahoma (formerly known as Kiowa-Apache). He grew up in LA, the son of a Navajo man who had been a child actor, playing opposite Jimmy Stewart in the 1950 Western *Broken Arrow*. Jon took a much different path, getting involved in ROTC as a young man and then becoming a police officer. He was top of the class at the police academy and won so many awards that the academy actually had to change the awards categories so that other cadets could win some too. He moved to the Navajo Reservation in search of work and applied to be a Navajo Ranger without even knowing what one was. But he was hired, largely based on his answers during the interview about how to deal with threats. They sent him to dig a uniform and leather duty belt out of a bin of used uniforms, gave him a badge and gun, and put him into service.

Jon worked in many branches of resource management and law enforcement. He was even an EMT—the only Navajo Ranger ever certified, to my knowledge. But when I met him, he was focusing primarily on archaeological enforcement, dealing with things like defacement of ruins and pot hunters stealing antiquities from archaeological sites. He had created his own enforcement program under the archaeological department, seeking out Congressional funding for a program entirely devoted to the protection and preservation of archaeological resources. Before that, there wasn't anything in place to serve this specific need. Of course, archaeological resources are an essential part of the reservation. Jon believed someone needed to be there to protect those sites and resources for future generations. There were a few other individuals involved, but he was the driving force behind the program.

It wasn't only law enforcement that we bonded over. We found that we both loved art and photography, as well as Native American traditions. Jon actually performs in Native American ceremonial dances, complete with all the traditional regalia. He belongs to a tribal warrior society that carries out these ceremonial dances. But also, like me, Jon is a huge music lover and an accomplished guitar player and singer. We share a common love of all things guitar—guitars, amplifiers, and accessories. We found so many things to bond over, which slowly turned our partnership into a friendship, one I still cherish today.

Jon and I worked well together, not only because of our similar backgrounds but because of the ways we were different. Our personalities and styles of investigation complemented each other, enabling us to approach a case three-dimensionally. Jon was good at looking at cases from a big-picture point of view. He tended to be good at abstract and dynamic thinking. In contrast, I was detail-oriented and analytical, loving my checklists and reveling in the minutiae of the work. Jon—who has a good sense of humor—liked to say that we were a bit like Oscar and Felix from the 1970s show *The Odd Couple*, creating a symbiosis from our different working styles and preferences. In that show, the actor Jack Klugman played Oscar, and Tony Randall played Felix. Oscar was the easygoing, messy slouch and Felix was the uptight, overly organized, obsessive-compulsive cleaner. Jon is certainly no slouch, but he's right that *The Odd Couple* perfectly captures the dynamic of our partnership.

It was a godsend to have someone I trusted so completely for a partner. I had started my career during a tumultuous time in law enforcement, when agencies across the United States were rapidly adjusting to a charged political climate. Particularly after the events of 9/11, all law enforcement agencies across the United States went through tremendous changes, and the Navajo Rangers were no exception. In the past, the Rangers hadn't been heavily involved in public safety. Natural resource agencies don't typically do tactical operations and SWAT; they stay within their niche of interpretation and park maintenance. That's why it was so unusual that I was given permission to participate in the Four Corners Manhunt.

But things had changed, and now all law enforcement were being trained in special operations. This hugely impacted our department and my own career. Chief Butler insisted on all Rangers being trained in SWAT and formed a seven-man SWAT team. I had actually been accepted to go to the Federal Law Enforcement Training Center (FLETC) Criminal Investigator Training Program at Glynco, Georgia, but there turned out to be a more pressing need for weapons specialization. One of the Navajo Police firearms instructors wanted me to be trained and certified as a firearms instructor, basically so I could assist him. So, I was sent to be trained as a firearms instructor instead of a criminal investigator. Firearms instruction would become a major facet of my law enforcement service, and over the course of my career as a Navajo Ranger I would always be grateful for the confidence my expert marksmanship gave me.

In 2002, the Winter Olympics took place in Salt Lake City, Utah, so the Navajo Nation had a huge presence and involvement. Before the Olympics had even started, there was an Olympic torch relay, and

Monument Valley Tribal Park was a major stop. They chose me to oversee special operations for the torch relay. It was an unprecedented amount of visitors and visibility for little Monument Valley. And I was in charge of all of it as a brand-new Navajo Ranger. Maybe I ought to have been intimidated, but I jumped in with both feet, eager to prove myself capable. Later, after the torch relay event had passed and the electricity that had been in the air began to subside, it was determined that a team of Navajo law enforcement officers would be used to provide security and to act as ambassadors for the Navajo Nation's Discover Navajo pavilion exhibit during its use at the Olympics.

Jon and I were chosen to be on a six-man security team and were commissioned as Utah State Police for the event. Our primary purpose was to provide security for the Discover Navajo pavilion, a large dome-like structure dedicated to Navajo culture and history. Its exhibits told of the Emergence, or the Navajo creation story, and shared important Navajo historical events. It also displayed the various arts and crafts that the Navajo are known for, including silversmithing, weaving, and basketmaking, as well as a full-size Navajo *hogan*, or house. The movie *Windtalkers*, starring Nicolas Cage and Adam Beach, was scheduled to release soon and was drawing a lot of publicity and attention, so there were actual WWII Navajo code talkers and the actors who played them in the movie present, as well as a display of their costumes. The Navajo Nation is particularly proud of the code talkers, who served the Marines during WWII. These men created an unbreakable code based on the unwritten and extremely complex Navajo language, which proved to be both effective and efficient, providing the Marines with a significant advantage in each of their operations throughout the war. The Navajo code talkers were considered critical to the victory at Iwo Jima. In 2002, there were very few code talkers still surviving, as many had already passed due to old age. It was an honor to be in the presence of these national war heroes and provide security for them.

Moreover, there was a heightened sense of alert nationwide following the terrorist attacks of September 11, 2001. Many were still on edge and reeling from fear after those attacks. I still remember hearing Air Force F-16s flying overhead during that time. The 2002 Winter Olympics was the first large-scale international event to be held in the United States following the attacks of 9/11, so tensions were running high and public safety was paramount. The security was coordinated under the direction of the US Secret Service with the assistance of the FBI. In preparation, our Ranger SWAT personnel were given a crash course in the history of terrorism and all the standard operating procedures and tactics related to terrorist threats and attacks. We were particularly alert to terrorism threats, with heavy surveillance of the surrounding area.

The duration of the event passed relatively quietly, although there were a couple of incidents that put people on edge. One incident occurred when an individual driving a vehicle refused to stop and sped through a restricted area. Another time I was on a break and had walked over to a nearby outlet mall and food court area to grab some lunch. Before I could get anything to eat, I had to deal with an incident involving an individual who had placed a large black duffle bag in an open area of the mall. This resulted in the area being evacuated and cordoned off and an Explosive Ordnance Disposal, or EOD, team being activated. So much for my lunch—I ended up providing security to keep people away from the scene. Later, the EOD team was ordered to stand down as the owner of the duffle bag came back to claim their property and sheepishly apologize for causing such a ruckus.

Providing security for such an important national event as a young ranger meant the world to me, and I was gratified to see many visitors come through the Discover Navajo pavilion and demonstrate the same awe for Navajo culture and history that I felt. Working events like the Olympics and later the Red Bull Air Race World Series in 2007 gave me a great deal of experience in working with the general public in very high-stress environments. Throughout my career, and Jon's too, we never followed the "us against them" philosophy that many law enforcement agencies employed—or the idea of "the thin blue line." Our view was that we were simply civilians in uniform and were sworn to protect and to serve our fellow man as public servants.

Around this same time, Chief Butler called a department-wide meeting to discuss an incident that would change the course of my career and my life. He said that there had been a complaint made against the Navajo Rangers by an elderly woman who lived in the Chuska Mountains. She claimed to have witnessed a Bigfoot step over her sheep corral and walk off with one of her sheep in its arms. When she reported the incident, two rookie Rangers were dispatched to investigate the case. They didn't take her report seriously enough for her liking, leaving her angry and upset. One of those Rangers was a known joker, a class-clown type who was always laughing and carrying on, so it wasn't too surprising that she ended up complaining about the Rangers' attitudes and behavior. But Chief Butler saw her complaint as an opportunity to address a larger need in the department.

"As Navajo Rangers, we are public servants, here to help and protect the public," Chief Butler said, narrowing his eyes at the offending Rangers. "It's our job to do that the best we can."

With his carefully pressed uniform, razor-sharp intellect, and decades of service as a law enforcement officer, the chief cut an imposing figure and commanded respect. This isn't to say he wasn't open-hearted or compassionate; he would always take time to talk to his officers. And he wasn't the type to sit behind a desk and leave the dangerous work for others. He was always part of the Navajo Rangers' SWAT operations. When he served as a Navajo Police officer, he had once responded to a call where his fellow officer had been shot and died. That was the worst thing a law enforcement officer could experience in the line of duty. It was a memory that weighed heavily on him. That's partly why he insisted on his Rangers being trained to the utmost. He had been Chief of Police for many years before coming to the Rangers, one of the best chiefs they had had in a long time. He was always out in the field and lending a hand where he could. That said, you didn't want to get on his bad side. The man was known to scold and lecture his Rangers like nobody's business—which he now proceeded to do.

He related the incident with the Bigfoot report, acknowledging that our department had failed the elderly woman. "From now on, reports like this one are going to be investigated properly, and you two guys"—he pointed at Jon and me—"are going to oversee these cases."

You might expect snickering from the other Rangers at this point, but it was dead silent in the room. After being reprimanded for a lack of professionalism, the other guys weren't looking to get into more trouble with the Chief. Besides, as Navajos, most of them took the supernatural seriously, despite the department's jokers. They were probably relieved *they* weren't the ones being assigned.

It was an unusual assignment, but at this point, I was used to being assigned anything out of the ordinary that came up and had learned to accept my orders without comment or questions. I also wasn't surprised that he picked us for the job. I had gained Chief Butler's trust early on in our relationship by my willingness to volunteer and jump in to help whenever I was asked, beginning with the Four Corners Manhunt. I volunteered thousands of hours of compensatory, or donated, time. His door was always open to me, and we had a good working relationship. Chief Butler frequently assisted me when I gave federal firearms instruction—and he usually earned a perfect score on his assessment with pistol, shotgun, and carbine rifle. Likewise, Jon was a trusted, well-respected ranger who went above and beyond his usual duties. We both had offices in the same building in Window Rock at this time, some of the few Rangers who did.

Besides, Chief Butler knew that, from a cultural standpoint, Jon and I were particularly well-suited for investigating cases relating to Bigfoot, ghosts, and witchcraft. We didn't grow up entirely on the reservation like a lot of the other Rangers, so we didn't have any hang-ups about the paranormal. We were, of course, taught not to leave our hair, nail clippings, or any bodily fluids where witches could find and use them, but we didn't grow up steeped in Navajo beliefs in the way many of the others did.

In every culture there are taboos—forbidden acts, behaviors, objects, and even thoughts. These taboos exist to prevent people from causing something bad to happen, usually as a result of a supernatural phenomenon. These taboos are often viewed as primitive superstitions by outsiders and are seen as ignorance or irrational behavior—at least until that person pointing the finger experiences the consequences of breaking a culture's taboo, namely a supernatural occurrence.

There are numerous taboos related to the paranormal in Navajo culture. Many taboos are a way to avoid contact with spirits. Children are taught not to speak idly of the dead or to use the name of a person who has passed on after the sun goes down. For the same reason, Navajos do not whistle at night, wash their hair or chop wood after dark, stack rocks, place ash at the base of a tree, or have any contact with owls, who are thought to be omens of death and spies for evil spirits. Spirits are to be avoided at all costs, and only a medicine man should attempt to deal with them. In Navajo culture, it's widely believed that if a person is experiencing something paranormal, it means that their life is out of balance and they are not in harmony with their surroundings. In light of these taboos, paranormal cases aren't something most Navajo Rangers would want to handle.

Generally, there is an underlying understanding of cause and effect—in a sense, the idea that for every action there is a reaction. In some cases, an action may create a curse or imbalance in harmony that a person will have to deal with in the future. Many Navajo taboos are rooted in the Emergence, or the Navajo creation story. Of course, taboos can change over time and be affected by many things, such as religion, culture, and societal influences. At the time most of these taboos came into existence, I don't think there were very many interracial marriages. The majority of Navajo were most likely full-blooded.

I am half Navajo, part Cherokee, and also part Irish descent, so in the back of my mind, I guess I always considered it was the Navajo part of me that avoided the taboos and the non-Navajo part of me that was able to deal with them, which sounds truly illogical, but it was enough of a justification or personal belief to me that it allowed me to move forward on these investigations and to stay focused on what needed to be accomplished. I guess I felt as though because of who I was and where I came from and how I was brought up, I too was a unique individual like many of the beings in the Emergence story that had certain abilities, powers, and protection. This personal belief, combined with a strong spirituality, allowed me to deal with these issues that most people from the reservation could not. It further allowed me to manage even the most traumatic situations, like incidents involving the loss of life or extreme injury, and to process these events without any lasting harm to my mental health.

Because of this mindset, I was happy to take on paranormal cases. I knew that paranormal events were not uncommon on the reservation, yet there wasn't a system in place to investigate and take them seriously. The cases tended to be ignored by police and other law enforcement officials, and those who experienced the phenomena were often called mentally ill or assumed to be drunks. This treatment left members of the community feeling alone and uncared for. I thought everyone deserved to be taken seriously, no matter how unusual their reports might be.

Besides, I thought it would be interesting to look into these cases and see what I could discover. That was part of the appeal of my job to begin with—every day was different, and I never knew what might happen when I put on my uniform each morning. Regular police officers were always going out on the same domestic violence or public intoxication calls, arresting the same people over and over. But being a Navajo Ranger meant constant change, problem-solving, and adaptability. I am curious by nature and love finding out how things work. Even as a kid, I liked to take my toys apart and put them back together. That's how being a ranger felt to me. This was just another opportunity to learn and grow. And I thought paranormal cases would be especially fascinating. I loved the 1970s TV show *Kolchak: The Night Stalker*, which was about an investigative reporter who investigated crimes with supernatural causes. The show was a predecessor to *The X-Files*, with episodes involving vampires and other creatures from science fiction. This assignment felt a little like getting to step into Kolchak's shoes.

Jon was excited to incorporate paranormal investigations into our duties too. He was a bit of a sci-fi nerd and certainly a known Trekkie. "Oh my goodness, we're going to be like *The X-Files*," he said after Butler had assigned us to the Bigfoot case.

Despite our excitement, we took the assignment very seriously and wanted to approach it with the professionalism it deserved. By this time, we were very familiar with the systematic processes and procedures of the National Incident Management System (NIMS) and the Incident Command System (ICS) that were implemented in law enforcement departments after 9/11 across the United States and had become standard in our department. Our ICS required meticulous planning and documentation to ensure the safety of our operators and the overall operation. Jon and I knew that we needed to try to establish standard operating procedures, or SOPs, along the same lines to guide our paranormal investigations, but we would have to be creative and adaptive in many cases.

When it came to firearms training or SWAT training, safety was always the number one priority above all other things. So, with investigating the paranormal it made sense that we adopt this same approach to the best of our ability. Safety would have to be the priority in dealing with these cases too, which was a great challenge, because with firearms we knew what the risks were and what needed to be implemented to prevent injury or death, but with the paranormal we did not know what the risks or safety concerns may be.

We assumed we would need to be able to protect ourselves against nonphysical attacks by entities that sometimes could not be seen with the naked eye, such as ghosts or spirits. Other entities related to witchcraft, such as shapeshifters, could cause physical as well as spiritual harm. It wasn't like we could use pepper spray, a baton, a Taser, or even a firearm on a ghost or something demonic. Because of this we turned to Navajo medicine and the expertise of medicine men to be able to protect ourselves and cleanse the personal space around us, as well as to keep ourselves in balance.

We knew we needed to establish a systematic approach to dealing with these cases and determine what our priorities would be and even what our overall objective would be. Since, in most cases, arrest wasn't a possibility and evidence may be difficult to collect, this required a lot of adaptation. So, given this understanding and the situation, what is it that we were going to try to achieve? We knew in the majority of the cases, there was a certain level of trauma and shock on behalf of the reporting person, or in some cases the surrounding family members. Much of our job would be to make them feel listened to and cared for.

Following the normal reporting system for our department was also a challenge. Jon and I needed to use the department's reporting writing system, but there were no codes to reference paranormal type cases, such as Bigfoot or witchcraft. So, we had to adapt and get creative. For example, we decided we would use something like "unknown animal" in a report for a Bigfoot case.

Jon and I always knew we would need to maintain the anonymity of the individual or family reporting paranormal incidents. However, sometimes rumors of the incident would spread like wildfire prior to it being reported to us. One great challenge was that an individual would report an incident and when we got on scene to conduct an interview, we would learn that the incident actually occurred days, months, or even years earlier. In typical criminal investigations it is critical to respond immediately and secure the scene to prevent any contamination of the evidence or the crime scene. Sometimes we would simply not be able to do this.

Therefore, much of our investigation would rely on the interview of the reporting person and others. Having obtained all types of investigation and law enforcement training in classes like Interviewing and Interrogation given by instructors from organizations as varied as the FBI and the Bureau of Indian Affairs Office of Law Enforcement Services helped greatly when it came to conducting the paranormal investigations. This training gave us the general tools, procedures, and templates that could be assimilated or modified to help us identify deception, determine credibility, establish the validity of a person's witness statement, or corroborate other information.

We put as much of this plan together as we could before beginning our first investigation, but much of it would come later, through trial and error. There simply was no guidebook for being a paranormal investigator.

We drove up into the mountains to meet an elderly woman and hear her story—a report of a large, unidentified creature matching the description of a Bigfoot that had made off with a sheep. Her home was about an hour's drive north from the Window Rock area depending on the weather and traffic. We made good time on the highway, the scenery of all the red rock formations and woodland areas passing in our windows. This route goes by a few small high-elevation lakes, including Aspen and Berland. There is another lake named Todacheene farther up the mountain. It is a beautiful drive. But once you get northeast of Crystal, New Mexico, and reach the turn-off that leads up the mountain, the drive can get pretty rough; it's a logging road that leads up into the higher elevation, so even though it's rocky at first, it is often very muddy.

But we were, of course, used to this sort of terrain and made it to the woman's home without incident. However, I suspected we wouldn't be able to do much for her. A few weeks had elapsed between the incident and our assignment to the case. That means we weren't able to secure the scene in a timely manner to ensure that evidence wasn't lost or contaminated. Sheep had gone in and out of the corral to graze, destroying any tracks the alleged Bigfoot might have left behind. The one thing we could do was listen to the woman and make her feel heard. We did our best to reassure her that she was safe and that we would be there to help her if anything happened again. As the higher-ranking officer, Jon took responsibility for interviewing her, and we both searched the heavily wooded area around her property for signs of anything that might be related to the loss of the sheep. But we weren't able to recover the sheep or find its remains. We didn't find any evidence of the creature she described either.

But I wanted to make sure I had done everything I possibly could for the woman, so I returned a few days later to perform more surveillance.

This time, I decided not to focus my attention on the corral where the sheep had been taken. For one, the area surrounding the corral had been completely decimated and continued to be trampled by the woman's sheep, so there was no remaining foot track evidence or impressions. I decided that I would concentrate on the secondary perimeter from the residence that was up to a mile or two from that location.

At first, the day was sunny with clear blue skies and only a few scattered fluffy white clouds. As I got up higher into the mountains, the world was so bright, and I was surrounded by natural beauty—trees and birds and wildlife. There was a very strong, clean, and almost astringent forest scent of pine and sagebrush. Before I began my surveillance, I stopped by the elderly woman's residence to check on her and to see if there had been any further activity, as well as to let her know I would be in the area until the following day.

I parked my patrol unit and let the dispatcher know that I would be out of unit but calling in every so often to let her know I was "Code 4," or okay, at least until she got off work at five p.m. It had been a long drive, so I decided to take a dinner break and dug around in my unit until I retrieved a container of MREs. By this point in my career, I was well used to these precooked packaged dishes used by the military as an immediate source of food for soldiers, and I'd figured out which variations weren't too bad. Some even had their own source of flameless heaters, so you actually got a hot meal. Most Rangers, if not all, carried MREs just in case. I remember this MRE consisted of a beef patty with a brown gravy and what was possibly mushrooms (you couldn't always tell with MREs). There was usually a powder to be mixed with a bottle of water for a beverage, as well as peanut butter, jam, and something similar to bread. Sometimes there would even be M&Ms for dessert. All in all, an MRE beat the hell out of starving, especially if you were way out in the boonies. I finished my meal and poured a strong cup of coffee from my trusty, beat-up old thermos, feeling positive and happy.

But by late evening that initial positive feeling had gradually changed, and I realized there was now a darker and almost ominous feeling in the atmosphere. I decided to take my first foot patrol and began walking through the tall ponderosa pines, the pine needles crunching loudly under the weight of my boots. Now the giant pines were beginning to cast long dark shadows across the landscape, and I began having the sense of being watched. All of my senses had begun to heighten, including my sixth sense, which was telling me to be careful and aware of my surroundings. As I walked, looking straight on, I would suddenly get the sense of movement in my peripheral vision, but when I stopped and quickly looked in that direction and intently watched, there was nothing there. Then I would hear sounds of something moving, maybe the breaking of branches or something walking through the thick layer of underbrush mixed with the pine needles that blanketed the forest floor. Again, I would immediately stop to listen, but nothing but an eerie silence met my ears, not even the sounds of birds or insects. This kept repeating time and time again, to the point of becoming frustrating and unnerving, a feeling of pins and needles spreading throughout my body.

Then, as the evening grew even darker, my mind snapped back to a movie from my childhood, *The Legend of Boggy Creek*, which I had watched at the local drive-in theater. It was a documentary-style horror movie from 1972 about a Bigfoot-like creature that had been frequently spotted in an Arkansas town for decades. As far as my senses were concerned, recalling that childhood vision of Bigfoot was like throwing gasoline on a fire. I remembered just how much this movie terrified me as a child of six or seven years old, having lived in the country in a heavily forested area. Now I discovered that the same ol' pit in my stomach, like burning coals, was back again after all these years.

Despite my trepidation, I continued to conduct my reconnaissance foot patrols away from the comfort and security of my patrol unit every hour or so, venturing farther and farther, deeper and deeper into the darkness of the forest, remembering all too well that this area was in close proximity to where the Bigfoot was said to have taken the sheep. It wasn't the best time to be wondering to myself whether or not Bigfoot was a carnivore. But no massive, hairy hands reached out of the darkness to grab me, and I continued unharmed through the long hours of the night until the sun rose again over the mountain.

This procedure continued for a few days and nights following Jon's and my initial response to the scene, and Jon conducted surveillance of his own; however, no sheep carcass or other remains ever turned up in the region, and no Bigfoot was ever encountered by me, Jon, or other Rangers that worked on this case.

One thing that did come from the Chuska Mountain Bigfoot case was that it set the tone for many other paranormal or supernatural cases to come. I would learn to listen to my gut instinct—my sixth sense. The outcome of this case also helped me realize that unlike in typical law enforcement cases, many times there would be no perpetrator in handcuffs or recovery of lost property, or even clear evidence of a violation or infringement. It wasn't like we could put Bigfoot in handcuffs and read him his Miranda rights. In many cases, the important thing was going to boil down to the manner of communication of the officers and the act of a timely response to the scene that showed the victim or reporting person in a very clear and overt way that the Navajo Rangers did care about the people that we served.

In some ways I was glad we didn't find anything. This paranormal assignment had come at me so fast. We'd been thrown into the deep end with this case, and we were just trying to learn to swim. What would we do if we did find something? I had no idea how I would proceed if I somehow managed to actually find a creature straight from legend.

I was skeptical but also open-minded. In addition to watching *The Legend of Boggy Creek*, I had read President Teddy Roosevelt's story in his book *The Wilderness Hunter* about a murderous creature now generally interpreted as a Bigfoot. This book was a memoir of his time hunting big game in Montana and Wyoming at the end of the nineteenth century. A trapper named Bauman told Roosevelt a story about going on a trapping expedition with his friend in a high mountainous region that separates the Salmon and Wisdom Rivers of Idaho and Southwestern Montana. The two ventured into a remote area with evil associations, where a man had previously been killed and half eaten by an unknown beast. During their trapping work, Bauman and his friend found footprints they couldn't identify, as if a bear had walked on its hind legs. After being menaced by the unseen creature overnight, they were terrified. But in daylight, their fears went away and they continued their work, heedless of the danger. That evening, Bauman discovered his friend at their campfire with a broken neck and three fang marks left in his throat. As a young man, I had found the story very convincing, especially as recounted by a former president and outdoorsman like Roosevelt.

Besides, there were tales of a similar creature in the Navajo creation stories, which told of a pair of twin brothers who slayed a giant monster that sounded a lot like Bigfoot to me. The monster, *Yé'iitsoh*, was associated with pestilence and disease, and the twins were heroes for slaying it. I knew that many other Native American tribes had their own Bigfoot-like stories that predated modern urban legends, as did cultures all over the world, from the Himalayan Mountains to Australia. Whether known as Bigfoot, Sasquatch, Yeti, or something else, in nearly all of these stories the creature was large, hairy, and walked upright like a man. Sometimes it was viewed as a protector and sometimes it stole livestock.

Certainly, the gears in my mind had started to turn. We might not have found evidence in this case, but it was clear that something was going on, though I wasn't sure what. I figured that if the creature was real, it must be some remnant of early humans, perhaps a type of Neanderthal that had managed to survive all this time in secret. In time I would come to believe differently, but at this point, I hadn't yet seen any definitive evidence to convince me that Bigfoot was real.

Going forward, Jon and I would have to make up our investigative protocols as we went along, working together to formulate a plan just like we always did for special operations. We knew how to track, secure a scene, and conduct an investigation; now we would simply learn to apply those skills to the paranormal cases that came in.

Looking back now, I do think that being assigned to these paranormal cases was my and Jon's destiny. There was something about me that seemed to draw the paranormal, from the unexplained events in my mother's home, to the skinwalker that chased my car, to the strange humanoid black smoke in the desert during the Four Corners Manhunt. It didn't matter if I believed in them—they believed in me. Maybe those entities sensed an openness and empathy in me, a lack of fear. Maybe my sensitivity to my environment simply made me more aware of them than other people would have been. Whatever the reason, I was exactly the right person to deal with cases like these. I was curious and open but skeptical. I wasn't afraid of the supernatural and trusted my Creator to protect me. I was ready to be a protector and a guardian, even if that meant protecting people from things I didn't yet understand. Later on, it would become my responsibility to spread the word about these events and let the general public know that these paranormal entities existed.

Although paranormal cases would make up only a small percentage of my and Jon's work going forward, from this point on, dealing with the paranormal on the Navajo Reservation was our responsibility. We weren't called it yet, but we were now The Paranormal Rangers. We were filling a need that no one else in law enforcement was able to fill, which was deeply satisfying to me.

And our investigation into the creature known as Bigfoot had only just begun. Within a year, we would be called to a community on the San Juan River, a forty-minute drive north of the elderly woman's home in the Chuska Mountains, where more than thirty individuals would report seeing a shaggy-haired, massive biped who matched the description of the creature that had eluded us in this case. The local law enforcement laughed at them, but Jon and I would discover that not only did they deserve to be taken seriously, but they truly had seen something not of this world.

THE FOURTH WORLD

All the People climbed out of the reed and emerged safely into the Fourth World, the Shining World, which would be their final home. But something was wrong. The floodwaters from the Third World still rose beneath their feet. Big Water Creature's head suddenly popped up through the opening in the reed. Her long, matted, curly hair floated on the surface of the water and lightning flashed from her horns.

First Man asked her, "Why did you come here?" Big Water Creature said nothing, but Coyote First Angry said, "It is because of this." He stepped forward and opened his coat and presented Big Water Creature's Two Children he had taken.

Turquoise Boy took a basket and filled it with Turquoise, Blue Pollen from Blue Flowers, Yellow Pollen from Yellow Corn, Pollen from Water Flags, and River Pollen. He then handed the basket to Coyote First Angry, who placed the basket between Big Water Creature's horns, along with Big Water Creature's Two Children. Satisfied to have her children returned to her, along with Turquoise Boy's gifts, Big Water Creature disappeared down the reed, taking the floodwaters with her.

The People now had a chance to look around them. They realized they were standing on an Island in the center of a lake, with cliffs all around as far as they could see. They did not know how they could cross the lake to the shore. But Water Sprinkler came and said he would help them. Water Sprinkler brought four Sacred Stones from the Third World. He threw each stone in a different direction to make holes in the cliffs, allowing the water to recede. Once the water was low, it created a path from the Island to the East Shore, but the path was too muddy to cross. Smooth Wind came to help the People. He blew a steady wind that quickly dried the mud and allowed the People to cross from the Island to the East Shore.

First Woman and First Man were ready to settle down in the Fourth World, but first they had to build a home to live in. This home was called a Hogan. First Man dug a pit and placed poles in it pointing upward toward the heavens. The main poles were two parts of the Black Bow. He cut another pole from the Great Male Reed. Then he cut one pole from the Female Reed. He covered the structure with dirt and grass. First Woman used white corn that was finely ground, and the poles were gently and carefully powdered. Then cornmeal was sprinkled inside the Hogan from East to West. First Man then said, "My Home is now finished; it is Sacred and Beautiful. May the days to come be Blessed and Plentiful." …

CHAPTER 5

The San Juan River Bigfoot
2003

THE DAY WAS TURNING TO EVENING, AND THE SUN WAS LOW IN the sky. A Navajo mother told her young teenage son to go outside and run off the coyotes that were disturbing their sheep in the field below their house. They could hear the sheep bleating and running around, clearly terrified. The boy hurried outside, BB gun in hand, where he discovered that what was disturbing the sheep wasn't coyotes or feral dogs or any of the other predators typical to the San Juan River area, but something much stranger. He was running so fast down the incline that he almost didn't see it; he barely stopped himself from careening straight into it and slid on the steep incline, falling backward into the dirt. When he looked up, there was a massive creature standing over him. It was taller than a man, perhaps seven or eight feet tall, with broad, muscular shoulders. It was covered all over in dark hair and had canine-like teeth. It smelled like a wet dog.

The boy dropped his BB gun and scrambled back up the embankment to his mother, who called the local authorities to say her son had seen a Bigfoot. The authorities laughed at the report, even though others in the area had already called in to their dispatch with similar sightings. A story about the Bigfoot sightings even made it into a local paper, but the police still did not take it seriously or investigate the woman's report. Finally, determined to have her case investigated, the woman reached out to the Navajo Rangers, and we decided to use the resources we had to help her family if we could.

Jon and I drove out to the northeastern edge of the reservation to a remote area of patchwork green fields and flat-topped, dusty mesas, with the fast-flowing San Juan River snaking through it all. We marveled at the many valleys, arroyos, and light-colored mesas that dotted the landscape and breathed the damp, slightly fishy smell of the river in the air, wondering what we would find here. Our aim was to interview the family and see if there was anything to their claims worth investigating. We had no idea at the time that this would become our first big paranormal case, with Bigfoot sightings up and down the San Juan River in a rural area on the outskirts of Farmington, New Mexico. We figured it would go the way of the Chuska Mountain Bigfoot case, with us poking around and not finding much at all. But that's not what happened.

The boy was clearly still shaken up by his encounter. He had dark, wide eyes that teared up as he spoke, and his hands shook when he described what had happened. He said he didn't want to go back to the field or even go outside. He was traumatized. After interviewing him and looking around the property, we found obvious evidence of a disturbance that we couldn't attribute to ordinary animals or events. There were clear foot impressions in the muddy soil of the nearby riverbed, fourteen to eighteen inches in length and five inches wide, with clearly defined toes. Whatever had made the tracks had a five-foot stride, which meant it was absolutely massive. For reference, the average human's stride is only two and a half feet, and a very tall man might have a stride a bit over three feet. Many of the footprints were found among bullhead thorns, whose sharp, poisonous quarter-inch thorns I remembered keenly from those tormenting push-ups of my police academy days. Whatever had left the tracks apparently walked through the stinging bullheads like they were mere grass, leaving no trace of blood or injury behind.

Of course, we first had to consider the possibility that someone was out hoaxing or having a laugh; it's necessary to be skeptical when investigating paranormal cases like these. Hoaxes are not uncommon on the Navajo Reservation, as I found out later in my career. It wasn't unlikely that some teenagers had gotten hold of a Bigfoot costume and were running all over the area scaring people for their own entertainment. However, we found no evidence of outside disturbances near the footprints, which would have been present if someone had been impersonating a Bigfoot. The footprints had a clear starting point and a clear stopping point, and there were no tire tracks, ordinary human footprints, or other indications of human involvement nearby.

Tracking is something I have done all my life, an established part of the Navajo culture. As a young Navajo boy, you may be out herding livestock, and a sheep or lamb may wander off, so you would have to track the animal and bring it back to the flock. Or you might encounter the tracks of a coyote, bobcat, or mountain lion nearby, which could be a cause for alarm. Therefore, being able to identify animal tracks and disturbances and follow their paths was essential.

Tracking fugitives as a law enforcement officer is a little bit different because the person you are tracking can actively try to throw you off and may be attempting to ambush you to kill you. Typically, you will start at the last known confirmed sign (usually a shoe impression that is confirmed as belonging to the suspect). From there you are scanning in bands or rays or a grid pattern for any disturbance—in this case, the distance of a human stride or step away from the last impression. You may locate the next disturbance and the next and so on. Sometimes, like in the Four Corners Manhunt, the suspects will be walking on the surface of rocks to avoid leaving a shoe impression. But you may still find a disturbance on the surface of the rock. As Navajo Rangers, we're thoroughly trained in tracking, and by this point in our careers, Jon and I had many years of tracking experience between us, so it would be extremely hard for someone to fake the prints without us noticing.

Besides, the boy had clearly seen something out of the ordinary, something that truly frightened him. Due to his age and emotional state, Jon and I felt even more urgency to investigate. We felt that he could easily have been hurt by whatever he had seen, and we wanted to avoid that possibility happening in the future if we could.

We went door-to-door interviewing neighbors over an area of many miles. The residences in this area were spread out; most were a half a mile or more away from one another. The interviews occurred over a period of several weeks and involved a lot of driving around. In a typical criminal investigation, interviews are usually conducted in an interview room at the police department. In this situation, the interviews were conducted at each residence or sometimes in our patrol units.

The interviews for a paranormal case are, of course, different from those of a typical criminal investigation. First, the whole focus and structure of these interviews will be different. In a paranormal investigation there is no suspect in the usual sense. So, there is not going to be a suspect interview or interrogation. In a criminal investigation, during the interview of a suspect, the interviewer is trying to gain an admission or confession using interviewing and interrogation techniques. In a paranormal-related interview, the purpose is to document or archive a possible paranormal experience or event that an individual has witnessed. We might also need to speak to a family member for additional documentation. By this point, I had already realized that my role in an interview with the victim was more counselor than anything else. I needed to reassure the victim that I, as a law enforcement officer, cared about their welfare and was there to help.

In the course of our interviews in the San Juan River area, we uncovered more than thirty firsthand sightings of a similar nature. The sightings took place on different dates and times, sometimes even different years. This meant that we had to treat each Bigfoot sighting as a separate incident. Additionally, because there is very heavy foliage in and around the river bottom, a person at one farm might have had a sighting, while their closest neighbor didn't witness anything, even if something was clearly in the area. There was a wide range of ages of those who saw something—young, old, and all ages in between. There were many eyewitness accounts of Bigfoot or of the gigantic footprints the creature left behind. Some reported their livestock being disturbed or even killed. There was one report that said it looked as if something had torn the wool right off their sheep's backs.

Reports were many and varied, and some of them were genuinely shocking. We had to perform a kind of triage, focusing only on the most important, compelling accounts. Some of the reports sounded more like the shapeshifters associated with witchcraft, but dozens of people had had an experience with a creature they described clearly as a Bigfoot. It was eye-opening for me to hear from so many individuals in one area who had experienced the same kind of event. One person showed us where a huge fist had crashed into the side of their trailer, leaving the deep impression of powerful knuckles. Another woman sighted the creature while driving, at first mistaking it for a hitchhiker before she realized it was covered all over in hair and didn't have any facial features she could discern. Many of the people had been frightened, even traumatized, and were now afraid to go outside alone. Others were merely curious. We soon realized that the sightings and accompanying incidents had likely been going on for quite some time. The witnesses' stories were each unique, but they all described the creature in the same way—bipedal, hairy, and huge.

Bigfoot was apparently loose in the San Juan River Valley.

A young mother named Brenda Harris had the most detailed narrative to relate. One night she was home alone with her young children while her husband was at work; she said he had just left for work around 10:30 p.m. for a graveyard shift. The windows of her mobile home were open since it was summertime, letting in a cool breeze. Around eleven p.m., only thirty minutes after her husband's departure, she heard something very heavy walking on the porch. It could have been a big dog or a mountain lion. But then that something started turning her doorknob. Again and again it rattled the knob, as if trying to get inside. Finally, gathering her courage, Brenda walked to the door and turned the deadbolt. When it clicked, the thing on her porch let go of the doorknob. She unlocked the bottom lock and swung the door open to the night. What she saw there left her awestruck.

A tall, black-haired creature stood framed in the doorway, staring back at her from the darkness. It was scraggly, not muscular, as most of the other witnesses had described the creature. But it was still terrifying.

Perhaps the creature was also afraid of Brenda because it darted off the porch, running west.

Brenda relocked the door and shut all the windows, which proved wise because thirty minutes later, the creature came back and repeated its curious behavior. This happened again and again throughout the night until the sun finally rose and the creature disappeared.

Once day broke, Brenda and her children went outside to investigate. They found a huge footprint outside her home, just behind her daughter's bedroom. It was the same kind that we found during our initial search of the area, approximately eighteen inches long and

four inches wide. With a footprint that big, she realized that the creature could have torn the door off its hinges if it had wanted to. Shaken
and determined to get evidence of what she'd seen, Brenda set up trail
cameras outside her home.

She captured something extraordinary. In the nighttime footage,
a small Bigfoot, perhaps a juvenile, seems to suddenly appear—as if
shooting up from the ground—beside an aboveground swimming pool
before running off to the west, in the same direction as the creature
that had been on her porch, perhaps running toward the river and the
shelter offered there. This didn't appear to be the same individual
that came to her door since it was a different size, but it was otherwise
nearly identical.

Did this mean Bigfoot was not a singular creature—one unique
cryptid, as the urban legends seem to suggest—but, in fact, a species of
paranormal being, with several individuals running amok in the area?

Brenda was electrified by the discovery. When she heard that her
neighbors had had Bigfoot experiences of their own, she decided to
help. They told her that a Bigfoot had broken into their horse corral,
rending metal and tin as if they were paper, so Brenda put up cameras
there too. She captured a silhouette that matched their description—
tall and shaggy-haired, standing eerily motionless outside the corral.

I was intrigued and concerned by these reports, but I wasn't yet
convinced. There might turn out to be a perfectly rational explanation
for what people had seen. But whatever was going on, it certainly war-
ranted investigation. If nothing else, we needed to demonstrate concern
to the citizens who were affected, especially after they'd been laughed
at and ignored by other local authorities. They wanted to know what
was going on, and we felt they deserved any answers we could give.

After completing our interviews and initial fieldwork, Jon and I put
together a three-day operation that included overnight surveillance.
It was a seven-man tactical team consisting of ourselves, four Navajo

Rangers with SWAT experience, and one Ranger from Special Assignments who had a military background and who frequently worked with our chief. We also brought along my cousin, Tony Milford Jr., who is an audiovisual specialist and camera operator who has worked with many well-known organizations and individuals such as National Geographic, the Travel Channel, Jamie Oliver, and Coolio. Tony already had an interest in the paranormal and was eager to capture video and audio recordings of the creature the local residents had witnessed. We brought along weapons and tactical equipment, including night vision and thermal technology. The eight of us spent Friday through Sunday in the San Juan River area, with many of us staying overnight, performing foot patrols and tracking along the river.

There's a saying about the Navajo Rangers that my partner Jon is fond of using: "Two Rangers together, that's a convention." Because we were so few in number and spread out over the 27,000 miles of the reservation, it was extremely unusual to see several Rangers together working on a single case. Our tactical team for this operation included Rangers from other parts of the reservation, who had to drive a long distance to participate. Of all the paranormal investigations I would be a part of over the years, this one involved the most department personnel. It was a massive undertaking, requiring a great deal to coordinate.

Additionally, in order to follow the national law enforcement mandates for planning and documentation, we had to consider scene security, which involved securing the scene of our operation; protocols for weapons, such as when it was acceptable to have a loaded chamber on our long guns; specialized equipment such as GPS, night vision goggles, scopes, and binoculars, as well as more mundane ones like camping supplies, bedrolls, tents, and food; preparation for weather and terrain, as well as wildlife hazards such as insects, scorpions, and snakes; and task assignments and evidence collection, photography, interviews, and the like. Accounting for all of these elements required a lot of work in addition to the actual performance of the operation. Simply making sure we could get all of our guys fed and find a place for them to safely sleep required a great deal more forethought than I had imagined.

But we finally got everything squared away, and each of our team members was given his assignment and instructions—one was assigned an observation point and directed to use either binoculars or night vision goggles, depending on the time of day. Another was given a digital recorder, and another was assigned to take notes. The search for Bigfoot had begun. We plunged into the thick Russian olive and tamarisk along the base of the San Juan River, looking for the supposed Bigfoot himself or any evidence of his passage through the region. My heart beat fast at the prospect of getting to see an actual Bigfoot. Even though adrenaline was coursing through my veins, I tried to remain calm and focused on our objective.

Performing a special operation at the base of the San Juan River took me right back to the Four Corners Manhunt—the heat and humidity, stinging and biting insects, and the claustrophobic atmosphere of the high brush, combined with the palpable sense of danger that always accompanies such a mission. There was a strong sense of vulnerability and uneasiness among our team, especially as the sun sank below the horizon and the sounds of nighttime New Mexico began to rise. Frogs chirruped and croaked, and birds whistled and sang. Animals moved unseen through the brush, each on a hunt of its own. But we were mostly silent. When you're on this type of operation, you are constantly listening for sounds that don't fit—ones that can't be identified as local known wildlife, domestic animals, or other ordinary sounds. Additionally, you don't want to risk giving up your location. So, most tactical operators speak very little and use hand signals to communicate when necessary.

The temperature plummeted, drying the sweat on our skin and leaving a shivery cold where the day's heat had been. Being out there in the dark, it was hard not to tense up, every nerve taut and expectant, just waiting for something to reach out of the dark and grab you by the throat. After all, it was clear that whatever we were seeking was big and strong. Something ten feet tall, four feet wide, and built like a tank—as many of the local residents described the creature—would have no trouble throwing us around. Its footprints were massive, and we continued to find new ones during our reconnaissance, meaning that the creature was out there in the river bottom with us.

Even more unsettling, during our patrols along the river on the morning of perhaps the second or third day, we found evidence to suggest that the Bigfoot we sought knew we were there and didn't want us searching for it. As we moved stealthily along the river, perhaps twenty or so feet from the water, we came upon a section of a log blocking the path we had been using for the past few days. It was about ten feet long and three feet in diameter, weighing over a thousand pounds. Something had picked it up and moved it to block the path. It had clearly been moved during the course of our operations since we had regularly been using the path. It wasn't close enough to the river for the water to have moved it. Judging by the indentations in the soil, the log was clearly picked up and moved from one spot to another—certainly no human feat, considering the immense weight of the log and the muddy terrain. It had been moved from an area near some trees and apparently purposefully relocated to the path. A person or even many persons could not have moved the log. It would have taken a backhoe to lift and move an object that size and weight, but you could not have used a backhoe in that location as it was too muddy. The area around the path was like a bog, covered in vines and plants. Besides, there were no mechanical track impressions. There was no evidence of *anything* mechanical or human moving the log.

I'll admit that my internal response involved a lot of *What the . . .* followed by expletives. I knew that no one on our team had done this, that there was no one else anywhere near here who could have done it, and that there were no tools or equipment in the area that could have been used. So how had the log been moved? The only answer was that the creature we sought had done it, a realization that genuinely shocked me. This finding was the moment I realized what we were up against. It was now clear to me that we were truly on the trail of a creature that might be as intelligent as it was enormous, and that it was just as aware of us as we were of it. It could step into our path at any moment, using the same strength that had moved the log on our much frailer forms. It was only wise to be afraid. But my training had taught me not to give in to the fear—and besides, we were armed to the teeth.

We tracked the creature as stealthily as we would a human fugitive, moving like shadows through the bush, our weapons at the ready. As strange, apelike and grunting calls—more like those I'd heard on the Discovery Channel than ones I was used to hearing on the Navajo Reservation—echoed through the landscape, Tony recorded them. But it felt like as soon as you stopped to really listen, the calls would cease and everything would go quiet again. We took photos and videos of the creature's tracks and made plaster casts of the footprints. Signs of the supposed Bigfoot were all over the area, but we never saw the creature ourselves.

We found a tuft of hair caught in a barbed wire fence, which the creature had stepped or climbed over, judging from the tracks it left behind. The hair bundle was about three to five inches long and contained black, white, and grayish strands. Jon sent it straight off for DNA analysis. The lab was unable to identify the creature, sending back the result "Unknown Carnivore." That stood out to me because the DNA database has animals from all over the world. If this had been an ordinary, known animal, they should have been able to identify it, especially since the hair sample had tissue attached to the root end, which usually ensures a good DNA match.

By this point, I was more than convinced that we were tracking a paranormal creature. The combination of witness testimony and physical evidence added up. It was clearly a biped creature of tremendous size and strength, unidentifiable by the usual scientific means. I was sure it was the cryptid known variously as Bigfoot, Yeti, and Sasquatch, though where it came from and what it wanted, I couldn't say. Was it simply hungry and looking for a meal? Was it curious about human beings and their dwellings? Did it wish my team and the local residents harm or only want to go about its own business undisturbed? Unfortunately, I truly didn't know.

With our evidence collected and documented, we had done all we could. It was time to close the case, even if Bigfoot remained on the loose. I do know that the boy's family was very appreciative that we came out to their home and attempted to capture evidence of this thing. But ultimately, the Rangers simply could not continue maintaining a post there. The family had a difficult decision to make about whether to stay or move somewhere the boy would feel safer. I don't know what choice they made, but given the economic precarity of life on the Navajo Reservation, I suspect they chose to remain.

Because of the effort to protect families and individual anonymity, there was no big public announcement of any of the findings or a front-page newspaper article. Each individual case remained compartmentalized. We did follow up by speaking to several families in the immediate area. But what could we tell them? It wasn't like we had captured a Bigfoot and had it in custody. For most community members at that time, it was enough that the department cared enough to send officers out into their community to try to ensure their safety.

I hoped they were safe and that nothing worse than a little fright would happen again. But I found myself considering that we didn't know what these creatures' sensory capabilities were—ordinary ones like hearing and smelling, or even additional paranormal ones. We had no idea what they were capable of. Did they have noses like bloodhounds? Were they capable of complex decision-making and planning? Did they have the power to appear and disappear at will, like that juvenile Bigfoot that seemed to magically appear in Brenda Harris's footage?

I had more questions than answers at this point, yet I still felt much as I did after the Chuska Mountain case. I figured that these Bigfoots were regional, earthly beings who migrated throughout the territory, remaining mostly unobserved by humans and eluding capture. However, I had begun to consider more seriously the connections between the Navajo stories of giants and what we were seeing. What if the Bigfoots weren't of his world? What if they came from somewhere else, perhaps from outer space?

I would continue to ponder these questions without reaching any real conclusions for many more years and through several more Bigfoot cases, which occurred fairly regularly for the remainder of my career. The San Juan River Bigfoot case was over, but my time searching for Bigfoot had hardly even begun.

YÉ'IITSOH AND THE HERO TWINS

It was during the time of the Separation of Men and Women during the Third World that Women had pleasured themselves with objects. Now, in the Fourth World some of those Women were with child. They gave birth to children with unnatural, disturbing bodies: a child with feathers on its shoulders, a headless child with hard skin and a pointed neck, and twins with no limbs and no head and depressions like eyes on its torso. A council of the People met and decided these children should not be allowed to live. They were abandoned in arroyos, alkali pits, and the chasms of cliffs. The People thought the children would die from the elements, but all of them survived, becoming Monsters that haunted those places and terrorized the People in their travels.

The last of these Monsters was birthed by a Woman who was impregnated when she placed a rock inside her Womanhood and Jóhnaa'éí, the Sun, sent a sunbeam into her to quicken it to life. A child grew in her womb. After nine days she gave birth to a very large, strangely formed child. Because she didn't know who the father was, she decided to abandon the child to die. She took the child and left it in a steep, rocky place. Jóhnaa'éí, the Sun, saw the abandoned child and knew he was the father. As the child grew, he watched over it and protected it, but he never showed himself to the child. The child grew to be a very large, angry, mean, and violent Monster known as Yé'iitsoh, the Big Giant.

Yé'iitsoh and the other Monsters hid along paths that the People traveled and killed and devoured many travelers. The Monsters became the bane of the People's existence; their weapons were useless against these Monsters, and they had no way to protect themselves. They lived always in terrible fear.

The People sought the help of the Holy People, who provided them with Changing Woman, a turquoise figure brought to life by the Wind. She gave birth to the Two Hero Twins, whose conception was steeped in mystery. The Holy People took the boys and made them train hard to become strong and run fast. Each day they were tested for strength and speed. The Holy People used switches made of Mahogany to whip the boys anytime they grew tired and ran too slowly. Each day the Holy People forced the Twins to train harder and harder, until they were tested and had achieved what the Holy People had intended, to be stronger and faster than all others.

The Twins were given bows and arrows made by First Man, and they traveled away to hunt. They tried to shoot several black birds—a Raven, a Vulture, and a Magpie—but their arrows missed. When they reported this to their Mother, Changing Woman, she scolded them and said the birds were spies for the Monsters. She warned the Twins that the Monsters knew about them now and they must stay hidden.

Soon, Changing Woman climbed to the top of a mountain and saw many Monsters coming toward the Village. She made four Sacred Hoops and cast them in each of the Four Directions. This gave them protection for the night. That night the Twins whispered to each other that the Monsters must be looking for them and that they must leave so that the others would be safe. Before daybreak, they ran down the Holy path to the East.

The Milford Family: my father, Stan; my mother, Emma; my older sister, Deborah; and one-year-old me at our home in the Bureau of Indian Affairs teacher housing in Hunters Point, Arizona, 1967.

BOTTOM: Two-year-old me wearing my father's chief headdress, which was part of his regalia for Native American dance performances or powwows, 1968.

LEFT: My father, Stanley Milford Sr., performing a Native American hoop dance in Tahlequah, Oklahoma, likely after a powpow or parade. The modern hoop dance is used by dancers from various North American tribes and is not specific to the Navajo. In fact, a member of the Jemez Pueblo tribe, Tony White Cloud, is known as the founder of the modern hoop dance.

LEFT: My Navajo Ranger uniform in approximately 2010. The[ ]are sergeant insignias on my collars and a SWAT commande[ ]pin on my left shirt pocket, signifying that I was the comman[ ]of the Ranger SWAT team.

ABOVE RIGHT: Taking my law enforcement oath, alongside about twenty-five to thirty other officers, at the US Indian Police Academy in December of 1997 at age thirty-one.

RIGHT: An actual page of the Navajo Treaty of 1868 on its one hundred fiftieth anniversary at the Navajo Nation Museum in Window Rock, Arizona. This treaty allowed for the return of the Navajo to their homelands after they were held in captivity at Bosque Redondo, New Mexico, following the forced Long Walk. This was the first time the Treaty was returned to the Navajo Nation and its people to be displayed to the public. The document's value is priceless. I was honored to be the law enforcement officer chosen to provide protection at its exhibition.

At the helm of a seventeen-foot Lowe patrol boat on the San Juan River during an operation to recover the missing body of a person who had drowned. Hours later, while my partner Lt. Jon Dover and I were camped out for the night, we saw what could only be a UFO, based on its flight pattern and speed.

RIGHT: Escorting a spelunking team into the abyss near Marble Canyon to allow scientists to map out the interior of this cave using a computerized system of lasers.

BOTTOM RIGHT: At work on a special assignment providing security for a vaccine shipment. We were heavily armed due to the risk of theft from cartels and militias.

BOTTOM: My Ranger Patrol Unit provided my transportation throughout the 27,000 square miles of the Navajo Reservation. Here it is near Satan Butte in Arizona, a potential paranormal hotspot, during an investigation into a case involving both UFOs and skinwalkers.

Taking on a new challenge in 2019. After I retired from the Navajo Rangers, I was sworn in as a senior investigator in the White Collar Crime Unit.

BELOW: My partner Lt. Jon Dover and me around the time of his retirement in 2010. Jon and I worked together in an official capacity for about twelve years; ten of those with the Special Projects Unit, under which we investigated paranormal cases.

Bigfoot track, plaster cast from an official case that I investigated with the help of my cousin Tony Milford Jr. at Tsaile, Arizona. We commonly made plaster casts of Bigfoot impressions; this one is fairly representative of casts taken in other investigations.

A Bigfoot track, or foot impression, also documented at Tsaile, Arizona. Along with creating plaster casts, we would photograph the Bigfoot tracks during our investigations. They frequently measured between fourteen and eighteen inches.

A tuft of hair found during the San Juan River Bigfoot case that was sent for lab analysis. The result returned as "unknown carnivore." This was significant because the DNA database has animals from all over the world, so they should have been able to identify it—especially since the hair sample had tissue attached to the root end, which usually ensures a good DNA match.

A thermal photograph from a Bigfoot case. Along with taking regular photographs of evidence, we frequently took thermal photographs using a thermal camera and software in order to provide a reference between temperature variations.

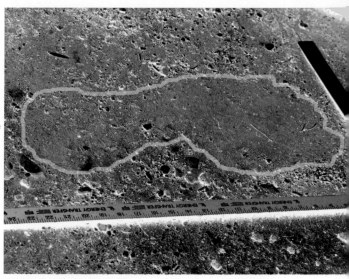

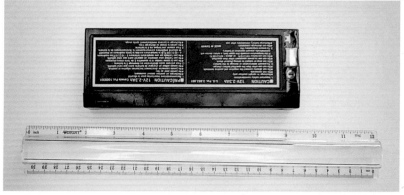

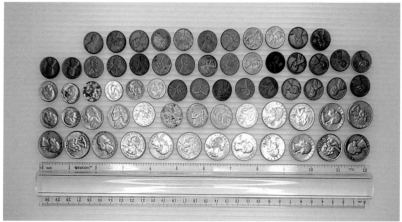

ABOVE: A battery thrown by an unseen force during a haunting investigation at an office in Window Rock, Arizona, in 2010. It suddenly came flying across the room and slammed into a cubicle wall.

BOTTOM: Sixty-six apported coins collected during a haunting case at an office in Window Rock, Arizona. Some coins appeared out of thin air in several rooms, falling to the ground and spinning, while others seemed to be thrown with force. All sixty-six coins landed heads-up.

A twelve-inch butcher knife at my cousin Tony's house following the Window Rock Haunting investigation. That haunting followed both of us home, manifesting with particular violence in Tony's home. This knife flew out of a butcher block, traveled several feet, and penetrated completely through a grapefruit in a hanging wire basket.

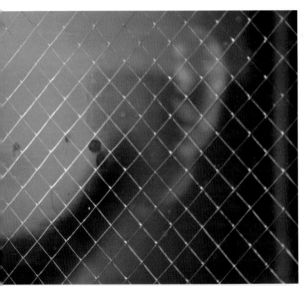

A ghost's face reflected in a window during the Window Rock Haunting case. It was unintentionally captured at the beginning of the investigation when we took photos for later reference. We only discovered the face later on, and we determined that it did not belong to any of the investigators.

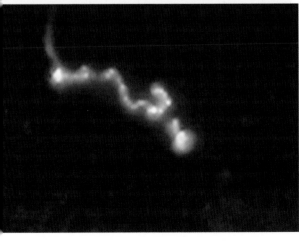

UFO photograph from an investigation near Satan Butte in Arizona, in which witnesses repeatedly observed a UFO. It was described as a large ship shaped like a spade, with red lights going across and several tendrils of light extending from it. The lights appeared frequently and looked like teardrops moving toward the earth. Witnesses also experienced skinwalkers and other phenomena on their property. The photograph was verified by the Mutual UFO Network's investigators, who assisted in the case.

Three illustrations, drawn by me, of some of the creatures I witnessed firsthand. Clockwise from the top-left, the first is Bigfoot, who appeared many times during my investigations, pictured here as seen in the forest near Twin Buttes, New Mexico, in 2014. The second is the Grey alien I witnessed at the foot of my bed during my own close encounter in 2014. The large black eyes, large head, small height, and long slender arms are what stand out in my memory of this encounter, coupled with the memory of a nauseating, rancid stench in the air. The final image depicts the skinwalker that chased my car down a dark road in Arizona in 1986. Each of these incidents lasted only minutes, but the details of the encounters will be etched into my memory for the remainder of my life.

They went to look for their father, whom they soon learned was the Sun. After a long and dangerous journey, aided by Spider Woman, they found him. The Sun said, "I will test you to see if you are my sons." He grasped them and threw them hard against the sharp White Shell Spikes on the East wall of the house. The Twins, holding the Sacred Hoop that Spider Woman had made and gifted to them, bounced off the wall unharmed. Then he threw them against the Turquoise Spikes on the South wall of the home. Again, the Twins were unharmed.

The Sun told them, "You must survive two more tests to prove you are my sons." He took them outside to a great Sweathouse and started a fire to heat large stones. As he did this, Wind came up to the Twins and whispered, "You must dig a tunnel to the outside and hide there."

The Sun commanded that they enter, which they quickly did. Then he asked, "Is it hot in there?" The Twins answered "Yes," as they hid in the tunnel they had dug. The Sun poured water on the hot stones, and they burst as the steam hissed inside the Sweathouse. The Twins soon crawled back into the Sweathouse. The Sun asked, "Is it still hot in there?" The Twins replied, "Yes, but not as hot as it was before." The Sun opened the door to let the Twins out.

The Sun said, "I guess you are my sons; come back inside the house and we will share a smoke." Sun turned to go back into the house. Wind came up to the Twins and said, "Careful, the tobacco is poisonous." Wind gave the Twins an antidote from Spiny Caterpillar to counter the effects of the poison. Sun prepared the pipe and drew smoke from it before he handed it to the Twins. They each drew a puff and exclaimed, "What sweet tobacco!"

Seeing they were unharmed, Sun said, "You truly are my sons. Why have you traveled here to see me?" The Twins replied, "We have come to see you, Father, for help. The Monsters are killing our People and destroying their homes." They asked their Father for weapons to destroy the Monsters. He said, "I can help you, but Yé'iitsoh, the Big Giant, is also my son. I will provide you with the weapons needed to kill the Monsters, but I will provide the first strike to kill Yé'iitsoh; he is my son too, so this I must do myself."

He gave the Twins protective helmets and shirts of armor made from flint scale. He gave them arrows of chain lightning and deadly sunbeam arrows. He gave each of his sons a knife with a hard blade and a broad blade knife made of stone. When the Sun left on his journey the next morning, he took the Twins with him. The Sun told them, "You are my sons. Be brave, and you will succeed in your war against the Monsters. In this war you will make your final passage from boyhood to manhood."

The Sun sent down a lightning streak to the home of Yé'iitsoh, and the Twins slid down the lightning into the canyon. They heard the heavy footsteps of the Big Giant, Yé'iitsoh, as the walls of the canyon shook with each step. The Big Giant bent down to drink from a pool of water and caught a glimpse of the Twins; he stood and stared at them for a long time. Then he shouted at them, but they did not understand what he said.

Yé'iitsoh paced back and forth and said, "What are the two beautiful things that I now see and how shall I kill them?"

The Twins shouted back, "What is the big beautiful thing that we see? And how are we to kill it?"

The Wind helped the Twins as they stood on the Rainbow path. The Big Giant threw his Great Black Knife and the Rainbow quickly rose; the deadly knife passed just below their moccasins. The Wind again whispered to the Twins, "Now keep low." Just then the Big Giant reared back and with all his might threw his Great Blue Knife at the Twins. The Rainbow dropped and the knife passed over their heads. Then, the Big Giant threw his Great White Knife, and the Wind told them "Jump left!" and the blade, with many razor-sharp teeth, passed to their right.

The Twins were about to attack Yé'iitsoh when suddenly a bright flash came down from the sky and struck the Big Giant on the side of the head. Heaven and Earth shook with the sound of thunder. The Big Giant staggered but managed to stay on his feet. Just then the oldest Brother shot a Chain-lightning Arrow at Yé'iitsoh, hitting him in the center of the chest. Then the younger Brother shot an Arrow made of Sheet Lightning, which found its mark, again in the Monster's chest. Yé'iitsoh fell forward on his hands and knees. The older Brother shot a deadly Sunbeam Arrow and struck Yé'iitsoh in the head. The Big Giant fell hard, face-forward on the ground.

The Twins approached Yé'iitsoh and saw the Big Giant lying there dead. The Monster who had killed so many was truly dead and could terrorize no more....

CHAPTER 6

Cryptids, Curses, and Cons

2010

JON AND I USED DISCRETION WHEN INVESTIGATING PARANOR-
mal cases and we certainly didn't advertise what we were doing, but
somehow people seemed to know. Word got around at the grassroots
level that we would investigate the cases other authorities wouldn't.
Paranormal events continued to happen on the reservation, and those
cases inevitably found their way to us.

Bigfoot sightings were one of the more common paranormal calls
that Jon and I received during the duration of my time as a Navajo
Ranger. We never had another big case like the San Juan River Bigfoot, but Bigfoot seemed to be always on the move in Navajoland. There
were dozens of Bigfoot reports made to our department while I was a
ranger. I wish I could remember all of those cases, but given the department's chronic understaffing, we were always very busy moving from
one assignment to the next, unable to dwell long on any one case, even

the paranormal ones. However, despite the frantic pace of our work and the many years that have passed, two Bigfoot stories in particular were significant enough to stand out clearly in my memory.

The first took place sometime around 2010 in Chinle, Arizona, a town in the heart of the Navajo Nation, where the water flows from Canyon de Chelly. An elderly, emotionally distraught woman called in to report a Bigfoot on her property.

I packed up all my usual gear and headed out, eager for another chance to investigate the creature known as Bigfoot. The San Juan River case had taught me to take reports of Bigfoot seriously, and I was curious about what I would find. Footprints? Hair? Would I possibly even see the creature for myself? It was a clear day and an easy hour and a half drive from my office in Window Rock. I went alone, but Jon would join me later in the day.

When I pulled up to the woman's trailer, several large dogs came running out to my truck, barking their heads off. This isn't at all uncommon on the reservation, where people rarely restrain their dogs. Luckily, I'm not afraid of dogs, and they seem to like me, always running right up to me to make friends and ask for pets and scratches. Growing up in Oklahoma, I always had both dogs and cats for pets and developed a deep love for them. So, I climbed out of the truck without hesitation and walked straight up to the porch, saying hello to the dogs as I went. The woman greeted me and took me inside, where there were even more dogs, only these were small, yappy lapdogs. She offered me a cup of coffee, which I gratefully accepted. As she busied herself with the pot and cups, I took a moment to observe her and her home.

She was a typical Navajo grandmother. She was probably in her early seventies. She wore the traditional dress of older Navajo women, or at least how they dressed when they were going into town. She had on a colorful blouse made of velveteen, in shades of maroon, with a matching skirt. Her gray hair was done up in a Navajo hair bun, or *Tsiiyééł*, which was tied with yarn. A Navajo woman's dress is never complete without being adorned with Navajo jewelry, so she also wore a turquoise and silver necklace, along with rings and a bracelet.

We settled down to talk, the lapdogs running around us and jumping up in my lap, and the woman told me her tale. She said that on the night of the incident, she was in her house watching TV as usual when the outside dogs started barking, really raising Cain. This set off the small dogs inside, who wouldn't stop barking no matter how much she shushed them. They grew more and more upset.

Finally, she got up from her comfortable chair and went outside to see what was the matter. There, beside her front porch, stood a tall, hairy creature—much larger than a human man. She said it had a foul odor like a wet dog, only worse. She raced back inside and locked the door. Her little dogs kept barking, but the outside dogs had all run away.

At one point, she dared to sneak a glimpse out the window by the porch, only to find a Bigfoot standing just on the other side of the glass. She was terrified.

She said the creature hung around outside her trailer for a long time. Finally, her lapdogs quieted. The Bigfoot was apparently gone. She called the dispatch the next day to ask for a Navajo Ranger to come check out her property. Some might wonder why she didn't call the police right away. You must understand that living on the reservation is not like living in other places in the United States. Elsewhere you can expect a police or law enforcement officer to show up in ten or fifteen minutes after a call. But on the rez, you're lucky if anyone shows up an hour after you call the dispatcher. That's if your call is even answered. The Navajo Reservation is huge, law enforcement is scarce and underfunded, and there just aren't enough officers and Rangers to go around. People learn to get by on their own and to have low expectations of receiving help. I was glad that the woman called the following day, rather than weeks or months later, which sometimes happens too.

Traditional in her beliefs, she called the creature *Yé'iitsoh*, referring to the giant in the Navajo creation stories. Many Navajos take comfort in the traditional stories since they provide a familiar, understandable basis for witnessing paranormal creatures. That was certainly the case for this woman, who was immediately able to grasp what she had seen and put it in a context that made sense to her. But that didn't mean she wasn't still extremely frightened.

I thanked her for sharing her story and promised to find out what I could. I headed outside to investigate, and was soon joined by Jon. When we looked around the area near the woman's house, we found ground disturbance and tracks similar to those in the San Juan River Bigfoot case. These were about sixteen inches long with clearly defined toes and heels, shaped like a human's foot but much larger. Some of the soil around the woman's house contained caliche clay, which becomes very hard like cement when it is dry. It would require incredible weight to leave the impressions we found—even a heavy, grown man wouldn't leave impressions deep enough to notice. This meant that we were once again dealing with an absolutely massive creature. The tracks started at the front of the house, then went around to the side, before heading around back. We took pictures of the tracks before following to see where they led.

There was a mesa behind the woman's house, and here the soil turned to sandy loam, where the creature had left even deeper, clearer impressions. The tracks led to the mesa and then up and over. It was incredibly steep terrain, and the average person wouldn't be able to follow the tracks without special climbing gear, which we didn't have. I stuck flags (similar to those used in surveying) in the earth to mark the creature's tracks and took more photos of its path.

The physicality of the evidence the Bigfoot left behind is something I thought about a lot whenever dealing with cases like these. Sometimes we think of paranormal creatures as ethereal, and it's not always clear whether a creature is present bodily—if you could touch it given the chance. For example, some people don't think skinwalkers are physically present, but are instead more akin to ghosts in their manifestations. But with Bigfoot it was always obvious—it left strong physical evidence wherever it went.

Jon headed back south, but I spent the night there outside the woman's house, watching for any signs of the Bigfoot from inside my patrol vehicle. I used my NVGs and thermal equipment. I never saw the Bigfoot, but I did catch its scent on the wind through my open window—a foul mix of wet dog and the sulfury stink of rotten eggs. The smell made the hair on the back of my neck stand up. It was a nauseating, foul odor. It reminded me strongly of the odor I experienced during foot patrols in the forest on the Chuska Mountain case, where the elderly woman's sheep was taken. It also reminded me of the uneasiness I felt there, the sensation of danger being close at hand, just out of sight.

I'm certainly no biologist, but the smell set me to wondering about the physiology and habits of Bigfoot. All that hair it has must get matted, and of course, like a wild animal, the creature likely never bathed. It might be covered in bacteria that developed a strong odor. It probably ate a lot of meat, giving it a carrion scent. Some wildlife have distinct scent glands that release pheromones that may smell particularly bad to humans but quite inviting to other members of their species. Any of this could account for its smell.

As the long hours passed, my thoughts turned to the creature's origins and intentions. I wondered how Bigfoot came to be, what it was doing here on the reservation, and what it would be like to come into contact with it. Each time I went looking for it, I felt like an explorer, even a bit like astronaut John Glenn, going into completely uncharted territory. There was the excitement of the unknown and the thrill of possibly finding something real.

That's what was different about paranormal cases as opposed to my usual, everyday ones. These cases made me wonder *What if?* They sent my mind whirring in all directions. I wondered if the Bigfoot had supernatural abilities in addition to being a physical being; for example, if it could pass through dimensions the way we pass through air. Could it make itself invisible? Is that why it was so rarely seen? Is that why I could smell it now but not see it?

The outside dogs stayed near, so the Bigfoot must not have been too close by. I shared my dinner with the dogs. They were mostly quiet throughout the night, with only an occasional bark and no signs of aggression or worry. Still, I felt uneasy; it was impossible not to with so many unknowns. I kept my carbine rifle in the passenger seat next to me with twenty-five rounds of ammunition. I knew that the caliber of cartridge in the gun likely wouldn't be effective for larger game, but it was what I had. Thankfully, I didn't have to test it. The Bigfoot stayed well out of sight.

The following morning, I reported my findings and the events of the night to the elderly woman, being completely honest with her about the size of the footprints, as well as the poor chances of actually tracking the creature down. I offered her what comfort I could, and she seemed relieved that I didn't believe witchcraft was involved, which she had been afraid of. To her, the dangers of someone using witchcraft against her were much more frightening than a Bigfoot out walking around. She was grateful that I took her case seriously and showed that I cared about her well-being.

I told her that I suspected that the Bigfoot might have simply been curious about her dogs, especially the ones inside, which it could surely hear yapping. Its behavior was so similar to what Brenda Harris had experienced with the Bigfoot that came up to her trailer along the San Juan River, minus the doorknob rattling. There really wasn't anything more I could do. I had used the normal techniques of law enforcement investigation up to the point that it was possible to do so in a case like this. After all, the Bigfoot couldn't be restricted or arrested for trespassing—it would come and go as it pleased. I had investigated and documented my findings, and that was enough for the elderly woman.

I went back out to see her a week later to check in and make sure she felt safe. She told me she had seen the Bigfoot outside her home again just a few days ago, but whereas during our last interview she had been agitated and frightened by the encounter, now she spoke calmly. Now that she knew witchcraft wasn't involved and that help would come when she needed it, she wasn't afraid of the Bigfoot any longer. Its comings and goings never troubled her much after that.

The other Bigfoot case that has stayed with me happened years later when I was the delegated Chief Navajo Ranger, after my partner Jon had retired. This one wasn't so different from the others, but I found it personally moving because it involved a young teenage girl who was genuinely traumatized by the events.

I was called out to Oak Springs, a small, rural community south of St. Michael's, Arizona. Our dispatcher said that her relative, a single mother with four children, had phoned in to report a Bigfoot sighting.

The town was quite a ways out and tiny, without so much as a convenience store. It was summertime, and all the schools were on summer break. The girl, who was thirteen or fourteen, was babysitting her younger brother. There was another teen boy there, as well as an older brother in his early twenties, but the girl was the one with all the responsibility. In addition to caring for her younger brother, she was responsible for taking their small dog outside to do its business.

That's what she was doing when she caught sight of something moving near their garden, which was full of corn and fenced in with barbed wire. As she watched, a creature emerged—taller and bigger than a man, with wide shoulders, covered all over in long, light-gray hair. It was about 150 yards from the house and watching her.

She grabbed her little dog and ran inside, screaming for her oldest brother, who hurried out of the house. He saw the creature too, as did her teenage brother, who was right on his older brother's heels. They all stood in the doorway, watching. The Bigfoot observed the three of them for a long moment before it turned and slowly walked away.

They took refuge in the house and called their mother, who was at work at the local government chapter office several miles away. Terrified by what she had seen, the girl refused to stay at home and begged her mother to come pick them all up. They spent the rest of the day at the chapter office with their mom while she worked, relieved to have some distance from the creature that had been lurking in their garden.

The mother arranged for me to come meet with her children. I met with the mother first, who let me know that her daughter was still very frightened. She was deeply worried about her daughter, who remained shaken up by the experience. The girl did not want to be at their house and wanted to remain by her mother's side at all times. Obviously, the woman had to work and could not watch over the girl and the other children all day. She desperately wanted to help her daughter feel safe again.

Next, I interviewed the girl. I felt her fear and anxiety so acutely that I knew I had to do anything I could to help her. Like the boy in the San Juan River Bigfoot case, her fear was still potent and very close to the surface, particularly when she was describing the creature she had seen. As we talked, her eyes were wide with fear. She cried at times, but it was restrained—not all-out bawling. She was terrified that this thing would return, especially when she was at home by herself. I assured her that no one on the Navajo Reservation had ever been assaulted by the creature known as Bigfoot, and that I suspected it was merely curious about people and their animals and homes. After all, not a single one of the thirty-plus people who had reported seeing a Bigfoot in the San Juan River Valley had been harmed by the creature, not even the teenage boy who nearly collided with it. She seemed to feel comforted by my reassurances and became less fearful after our conversation.

Next, I walked down to the garden fence where she had seen the creature, and I found clear Bigfoot tracks consistent with those I had seen before, as well as evidence of dogs and wildlife. A Bigfoot had certainly passed through their property, and I wouldn't be surprised if the creature returned.

Moved by the girl's fear, I went out to their residence two more times to walk the land and look for tracks. It was very flat land around their house, with mesas in the background. There were a lot of woodland-type trees down to the west of the garden, as well as some larger trees as I ventured farther up the mountain to the southwest. The terrain to the south was complex, with steep canyon areas nearby. There were certainly plenty of places a creature like Bigfoot might be hiding. I carried my carbine rifle to be safe, but I didn't catch sight of the Bigfoot. The second time I went out there, I heard a large animal moving in the woods, crunching through the fallen leaves and sticks, but of course, that was far more likely to be a mule deer, elk, or someone's livestock.

This case drove home for me, perhaps more than any other, just how traumatizing an encounter with the paranormal can be for people. It can leave lasting psychological scars and cause severe anxiety. Coming face-to-face with something so outside of the usual realm of human experience can utterly rock a person's sense of the world and their own safety in it. Thus, when they share their experience and their fears and are laughed at by people who ought to help them, their trauma is compounded, turning into shame and self-doubt.

By this point, my operating procedures for paranormal cases were extremely well established, and I knew what my primary objectives were: to make the individuals involved feel as safe and cared for as I possibly could and to document any evidence I found as carefully as I would the findings of a criminal investigation. The point was to take these citizens' cases seriously and treat them with respect while trying to get at the truth of what was really going on.

Of course, Jon and I were not always able to find evidence for reports of paranormal encounters. Sometimes there was clearly something other-worldly going on, sometimes there was a mundane and rational explanation, and sometimes we simply had to chalk it up to mystery. But investigating carefully and doing my best to get to the bottom of things was always a rewarding process, no matter the case's outcome. Sometimes the unlikeliest of cases provided an opportunity to help people in unexpected ways.

One such case involved a middle-aged woman who lived half a mile from Gallup, on the outskirts of the Navajo Reservation. She was convinced that someone was using witchcraft against her and feared that a skinwalker might be prowling her property. She had contacted every branch of law enforcement in the area, pleading for help from authorities in several counties, and no one would give her the time of day. She was at her wits' end by the time dispatch connected her with the Rangers. Jon and I went out to meet with her and hear her story.

She lived on a butte in a somewhat remote area, despite being so near to Gallup. Her home was a traditional Navajo hogan. There are male hogans, which are intended for ceremonial purposes, and female hogans, which are intended to be lived in. This was an eight-sided female one with a door facing to the east, between fifteen and twenty feet in diameter. The hogan had a low roof as such structures generally do, only six feet off the ground at the edge and ten feet at the center. Most hogans are made of logs or are covered in mud, but this one had a wood-frame structure. The hogan is a fairly simple house, with an opening at the top for a stove flue or to allow smoke from a fire to escape.

We interviewed her in Jon's patrol truck, with her in the passenger seat and me in the back taking notes. This might seem strange, but we frequently conducted interviews in our patrol vehicles. It provided a quiet place where we could easily record the interview, as well as giving us a subtle measure of control over the proceedings. When you enter someone's home, you are on their turf and more vulnerable to attack. But our patrol vehicles were a fairly neutral environment that we could nonetheless control.

Our initial interview took about three hours, and she was very upset for much of it, crying and afraid—both of the witchcraft and of being laughed at again. Of course, we had to ask her about her drinking habits and mental health; this was a routine part of our investigations. The woman didn't shy away from our questions, admitting to serious mental health issues and even bringing out a large paper bag of her medications to show us that she had been taking them faithfully. The medications were serious psychotropic prescriptions. She reported that she was separated from her boyfriend and wasn't close with any family members. Thus, she presented the perfect picture of the unreliable witness, and I wasn't surprised that the other law enforcement agencies had labeled her an EDP, or emotionally disturbed person, and laughed off her reports. But it was clear to me that something was going on, whether it was paranormal in nature or not. She was terrified and needed our help. It was our job to do our best to investigate her claims and concerns—to find out the six *W*s: who, what, when, where, why, and how. We would gather our information and let any evidence we found speak for itself.

The woman reported that she had left Gallup and moved to Phoenix several years ago, but she continued to travel between the two cities, returning to her hogan in Gallup when she was able to do so. On her most recent return, something was different. She kept finding little bundles of leather and twigs around her home. They were left in doorways and on windowsills, once even on the roof. She would frequently hear strange noises, like something was scratching or tapping on the door or side of the house. Sometimes the door handle would be jiggled. Often, she would hear something moving around on the roof, but when she went outside to look, nothing was there.

After we took her statement, we surveyed her home and the area around it. The only tracks we found were human shoe prints, which we followed toward Gallup, already beginning to get an idea of what was truly going on here. Local drunks and transients often walk into Gallup to buy cheap wine and liquor since they aren't able to purchase alcohol on the reservation. After they get drunk, they go looking for a place to crash. The woman's empty hogan had provided an irresistible place for them to drink and sleep.

This kind of behavior is a big problem in areas surrounding Gallup and other border towns where people go to get their booze. Vagrants and alcoholics tend to congregate in these areas. Sometimes they buy the cheapest wine and liquor they can, and other times, when they're really hard up, they make and drink a concoction known as Ocean—a mixture of rubbing alcohol and Listerine filtered through a loaf of bread. Alcoholism is one of the most difficult social issues plaguing the Navajo Nation, one I experienced firsthand with my own father. Of course, it often goes hand in hand with poverty. Just arresting the drunks isn't solving anything, and until the Navajo Nation and the US government get serious about dealing with the true root of the problem—poverty—nothing is ever going to get better. If people can't find jobs and work, they are going to drink. It's a situation I feel deep compassion for.

But, of course, in this instance all of our concern was for the woman being terrorized. We did surveillance around the property, which primarily consisted of foot patrols in the surrounding woods and watching for individuals around the area with binoculars. We also examined the bundles of leather and twigs she had found and took them with us to show a medicine man. He immediately laughed when he saw them and said they were phony, confirming our own suspicions. There was no witchcraft in these bundles at all.

The outcome of the case was this: These local drunks and transients had gotten used to using the hogan and didn't appreciate the loss of it when the woman returned from Phoenix. They decided to try to scare her off with the threat of witchcraft, which is something most Navajos take very seriously. They must have thought that if they terrorized her enough, she would go away again and they would have the hogan for themselves.

It was a true pleasure to be able to explain all of this to the woman and watch the relief spread across her anxious face. She had been so frightened and so alone, and being mocked by the law enforcement officers who ought to have helped her only made it worse. By dismissing her concerns as mere superstition or mental illness, they missed an opportunity to provide support and help to one of their citizens. In short, they failed to achieve the primary responsibility of protecting and serving.

Our presence at her hogan had another effect: the vagrants stopped bothering her. We never found any particular individuals who were responsible, but they must have been watching us from afar and got the message: Their crash pad wasn't theirs anymore. The woman's mental health seemed to improve somewhat now that she wasn't constantly being terrorized, and she was able to fix up her hogan and make it more of a proper home.

This was what Jon and I call a typical Scooby-Doo case, almost absurd in its fakery. But it was life and death to the woman, who would probably have been completely run off by those vagrants if we had not intervened. She wasn't at all offended to find out that she had been wrong about experiencing something paranormal—quite the opposite. Our debunking gave the woman her home and her life back. She later called the dispatch to express how grateful she was, and when I ran into her a few times, she let me know she was doing better and enjoying her home.

However, people aren't always so happy to find out that what they thought was a paranormal experience is something much more mundane. For some individuals, experiencing a paranormal or otherworldly event gives them a certain distinction in their own eyes, making them feel special. Or sometimes they are simply so convinced that what they have seen is paranormal in nature that nothing we would say could possibly sway them.

One of the most memorable examples of this happened around the same time, and in the same area of northeast Arizona, as the Old Man and the UFO case that's discussed in the next chapter. A grazing officer in a small community south of Ganado, Arizona, reported seeing UFOs on a nightly basis. Every night like clockwork, he said, the lights in the sky would appear, and they were surely something out of this world. I went out to take his statement and promised to find out what I could. He pointed out the direction of the lights he had witnessed, which could be seen through the bare branches of trees that had been badly burned in a wildfire that had recently decimated the trees in this whole region.

I went out at the time of night he said the lights always appeared. The trees were skeletal and eerie in the darkness, and indeed, I did see the lights that he mentioned. They too were eerie, rising up through the trees like fireflies. I found this very interesting and was eager to figure out where they came from. I went out a few times, and each night, just as the man said, the lights would appear. Puzzled by their appearance, I pulled out my night vision goggles in hopes of getting a better look. Next, I used my compass and maps of the area to identify exactly where the lights originated. To do something like this, you must first determine your exact location using a handheld Global Positioning System, or GPS. This device can give your location in various mapping coordinates, such as latitude and longitude or Universal Transverse Mercator, or UTM. Second, once you have your position, then you can determine a bearing in degrees to another location, object, or landmark using a compass. In this case, it was the lights that formed in the night sky.

What I found didn't involve UFOs or extraterrestrials at all—only some interesting science. On a map I determined that the lights were on the same bearing or azimuth as a nearby residential housing development. I traveled to observe the housing at night, which had streetlights that lit the sky above the area. The appearance of the lights occurred at the same time every night when the sky was clear. It was now obvious to me that the lights the grazing officer witnessed were from the residential area. They were merely ordinary streetlights. Normally, you wouldn't be able to see these lights from where the grazing officer saw them, but due to a temperature inversion the lights became visible and seemed to rise in the sky. A temperature inversion means there is a change between layers of temperature, with warmer on top and colder below, creating a barrier that lights can reflect off. Much like a mirage in the desert where water seems to appear on a hot summer day, the reflection of these lights tricked the grazing officer's vision into experiencing them as something otherworldly. I explained all of this to him, but he only shook his head and refused to believe me. He was sure he had seen UFOs, and no amount of rational discussion could convince him otherwise.

As interesting as the paranormal may be, sometimes there is simply a logical explanation for the phenomena that people encounter. My job as a Navajo Ranger—even as The Paranormal Ranger—wasn't to prove that the paranormal was out there. It was simply to investigate the cases that came my way and do my best to find the truth. It's easy to get a bit grandiose when working on paranormal cases—or too big for your britches, as my rural Oklahoman neighbors might say. But I truly did try to be like Sherlock Holmes when I investigated these cases, taking nothing for granted and doing my best to solve the puzzle. It was just as satisfying when that puzzle turned out to have a mundane cause as a paranormal one. The important thing was finding the truth.

Despite my commitment to Sherlock-like objectivity, I was never a coldhearted skeptic, and it wasn't possible to keep myself entirely separate from the paranormal phenomena I investigated. These cases had begun to change me, primarily by expanding my view of the universe and the possibilities of what life can be. I had always known that our universe was vast beyond our comprehension. These cases taught me that there is life beyond this little planet we live on—life so far beyond what we can imagine. From time to time, we get the results of that: UFOs, Bigfoot, and other entities crossing over into our realm, leaving evidence of their passage, and unfortunately sometimes traumatizing people.

More and more, I began to realize how limited we are as a species. Humans have delusions of grandeur, believing that we are the pinnacle—and the purpose—of creation. But that is laughable because we are nothing close. Humanity is like a little grain of sand on a mile-long beach, unable to grasp the vastness of the universe and the tiny role we play in it.

But realizing our insignificance in the face of a limitless universe didn't depress me. Instead, it expanded my range of thought and emotions. Investigating these cases helped to make me a better ranger and a better person. I became more apt to listen than to speak, eager to empathize and understand. I started making connections among different cases across the reservation, seeing larger patterns.

And I became more hopeful—that there is more to the world than what's in front of our faces, and that we could make our world better if we choose to. We don't have to have homeless people sleeping on the streets or children going hungry and doing without. The Earth could be a paradise, without pollution, without hunger. We could eliminate disease and poverty and live long, good lives. Opening my mind to the vastness of the universe opened my eyes to what was right in front of me, the needs of my community, and the possibilities of human life.

As silly as it might sound to some people, the very existence of Bigfoot and UFOs gives me hope and makes me dream—not only of the possibilities of their worlds, but also the possibilities of my own.

CHAPTER 7

The Old Man and the UFO

2009

GROWING UP, I SOMETIMES HEARD ABOUT UFO SIGHTINGS ON the reservation, from both family members and neighbors. My dad and uncles had stories to tell about lights in the sky above the Navajo Nation. My father once told me about an incident that took place while he was coaching softball at the Toyei Boarding School in Arizona in the 1970s, when a large silver cigar-shaped craft was observed hovering nearby. He said it had no engine noise, and he knew it was definitely not an airplane, helicopter, or blimp. He said he and the other teachers and students clearly witnessed this object, which he referred to as a craft or UFO.

I was also aware of the somewhat famous UFO incidents that had taken place in the Southwest and other places in the United States in the decades before my birth. One was the Lubbock Lights incident that occurred in Lubbock, Texas, between August and September 1951, in which a strange light formation was spotted by a trio of professors, among others, and was investigated by the Air Force. I read about the 1950 McMinnville UFO sighting, or the Trent UFO Photos as that incident is also known, in which an Oregon farmer couple witnessed and photographed a saucer-shaped UFO. Of course, I knew about the 1947 Roswell Incident, regarding a UFO crash and military cover-up. I also read about the Kenneth Arnold UFO sighting of 1947 that led to the term "flying saucer." A book I found in my father's library was *Chariots of the Gods?* by Erich von Däniken, published in 1968. This author hypothesized that ancient civilizations such as Egypt gained their technologies and aspects of their religion from extraterrestrial visitors. All of these events and the publications that recounted them certainly made an impact on me and made me wonder if other life existed in the universe.

Today I use the terms UFO and extraterrestrial in their most commonly accepted forms, just as I did as a kid: UFO, or Unidentified Flying Object, means an unidentified aerial object seen flying through the air, and extraterrestrial means a being from another world. These terms are serviceable and easily recognizable, though other terminology is increasingly favored by government and scientific agencies: UAP, or Unidentified Anomalous Phenomena, is another way to describe UFOs, essentially any object detected in the air or in space that we cannot identify or that moves in ways that are impossible for human-made crafts. EBE, or Extraterrestrial Biological Entity, is another term for extraterrestrial, meaning a biological being not from Earth. But these are just new ways to describe something human beings have been experiencing for millennia.

When I thought about UFOs as a kid, I always pictured the kind I saw on TV: disk-shaped, silvery metallic spacecrafts piloted by little green men in skintight suits. But in Navajo culture, extraterrestrials aren't thought of only in the context of science fiction; they are written into our creation myths. Many Native American tribes have legends about Star People, beings who come to visit Earth from time to time. The term Star People is a generic, anglicized English term that essentially refers to astral beings or extraterrestrials that originate from other worlds, planets, or dimensions. Some of these references may originate from a tribe's traditional creation or emergence stories. They are represented in the pictographs and petroglyphs scattered throughout the Navajo Nation, carved into red rock sandstone by Pueblo and Anasazi peoples.

Jon Dover and I had a good friend, Clifford Mahooty, who was a civil engineer as well as a wise elder of the Zuni tribe and a member of the Galaxy Medicine Society, the Kachina Priesthood, and the Sun Clan. Unfortunately, he passed away in January 2022, but Jon and I were fortunate to be able to call him a friend and benefit from his teachings on Star People. His knowledge of Zuni traditions was unparalleled. Clifford was taught by many elderly grandfathers and taught me that the Pueblo peoples who occupy or have occupied pueblos, such as the Zuni, Hopi, Acoma, and Laguna peoples, have a distinct and unique mythological-based view of the Star People. Clifford taught me that the Zuni tribe's kachinas, which are spiritual deities or gods, are actually representations of these Star People, describing them as similar to alien beings from other worlds or planets, originating from other galaxies and solar systems. The kachinas visited humans to bring them blessings and help. He further described the clan relationship system that showed a sacred medicine order. He also spoke of the Zuni Shalako, which is a series of ceremonies, dances, and a feast conducted during the winter season after the fall harvest. There are kachina dancers who participate in order to give thanks for the harvest. Their colorful ceremonial regalia is meant to depict the kachina deities and often reach heights of nine or ten feet.

Clifford showed me many photographs taken of the numerous petroglyphs and pictographs from the Zuni region and other Southwest areas.

He pointed out images of giant beings, which he associated with Bigfoot, as well as depictions of extraterrestrials and UFOs. These depictions are often called rock art, but Clifford taught Jon and me that this was an erroneous way of thinking. He impressed upon us that their value lies not in artistic expression but in historical record. Thanks to Clifford, we came to view petroglyphs and pictographs as a written record and an archive of real events. Jon and I do differ slightly in our interpretation. Jon views them as a complete and total picture, but I think their meanings are vast and variable because the same section of rock can contain depictions from totally different historical periods, representing the history of the Fremont, Basketmaker, Anasazi, and Hopi peoples. The meanings piled up over the centuries in the same way layers of rock are built over eons.

But Star People are not only a part of our history. There is a consensus among most tribes of the Southwest today that there are extraterrestrial beings who come to our world and that they have been doing so for a very long time, maybe even before human beings existed on Earth. Overwhelmingly, Navajos believe that the aliens come to Earth to benefit humans and to influence us to do good things and to avert war and conflict. This goes back to the traditional Navajo teaching of *hózhó*, or harmony and balance in life. So, for some Navajo people, witnessing a UFO or extraterrestrial is actually a deeply spiritual experience, harkening back to our creation mythology and traditions.

Still, a lot of Navajos are hesitant to share stories of UFO sightings openly. I have spoken to many elderly Navajos in particular who had UFO experiences decades ago that they never shared with anyone. Some are afraid of being considered crazy and shunned, while for others, the experience is far too personal to share. Thus, I was grateful when the elderly Navajo man who is the subject of this chapter was willing to trust me with his story, which has stuck with me for many years and significantly changed my thinking about the possibilities of extraterrestrial life.

In about 2009 or 2010, Jon and I drove out to a community near Ganado, Arizona, to meet with an elderly man who claimed to have seen both a UFO and the extraterrestrials that piloted it. He had reported the sighting to his local grazing official, who reached out to a Navajo Ranger who worked in the area. That ranger then contacted Jon and me, and we decided to investigate the case officially under our Special Projects Unit. This was one of those rare times that a supernatural event was reported in a timely manner. The old man had the sighting on a Saturday, and by Monday we were on location, with an extended interview set up for the following Wednesday.

On a cool, clear morning we met with the ranger and grazing official, then followed them out to the location, which was very remote. It was in a small town with nothing more than a gas station, and the old man's house was several miles out. The first thing I noticed was that the entire area had been decimated by wildfire, so there was no green anywhere, despite the numerous pine and oak trees in the vicinity. The bare branches of the burned trees thrust up into an empty blue sky for miles around, like a legion of skeletons marching through the landscape. The old man's home was, amazingly enough, untouched by the fire, despite being made of wood and surrounded by burned trees.

Given this environment, I expected to find the old man's home rather quiet and lonesome. But instead, there was a buzzing kind of electricity in the air as we pulled up to the residence. A few of his adult children and their families were visiting, and the old man's experience with the UFO had created a stir of concern and interest in his family. His own energy, however, was calm and measured.

The old man was a retired railroad worker and a typical Navajo *cheii*, or grandfather—about five foot six, with silver and turquoise Navajo jewelry on his wrists and fingers. He spoke slowly, in a direct and measured way with clear, sharp intelligence. Despite his advanced age, I wasn't at all worried about his mental state. He never used the terms UFO, alien, or extraterrestrial. He described what he had seen in straightforward and simple terms, translated from Navajo by the government translator we brought along. Here is the story he told. . . .

The old man was home alone one night because his wife and children had gone to visit one of his grandchildren, who was attending college in Phoenix. It was getting late, perhaps about midnight, when he decided to go to bed. As he was getting ready, he saw lights outside. Thinking they were headlights and that someone was driving up to his home, he walked out to the poured concrete patio to see who it was. What he saw instead was a UFO. It was spherical and about twenty-five feet in diameter. It was bright like the sun, an intense yellow or orange with colored beams of light strobing and flashing.

The craft flew slowly and deliberately around his home before moving a quarter of a mile away at the same pace and hovering above the tree line. Then the old man saw lights at the ground level below the craft. They were flashing and moved south from underneath the object, then back toward the craft, before gradually making their way toward his home. When they made it halfway to his home, one of his dogs, a little rez mutt, ran out toward the lights and disappeared into the dark. A few moments later, when the dog reached the lights on the ground, it yelped in pain as if kicked.

At that point, the old man became frightened and went inside his house and shut and locked the door. He watched from behind the curtains to see what would happen next. The little dog didn't reappear, apparently deciding it would be safer to run off and hide for the time being.

The lights approached his home, and he realized the light was coming from objects held in the hands of four beings. The beings were each about three feet tall, childlike in their proportions, with gray skin. Their heads were oversize, about the diameter of a basketball, and they either had large black eyes or were wearing goggles. He couldn't tell if the beings were naked or simply wearing tight-fitting suits.

The beings wandered around his yard and shone their lights on the ground as if looking for something they had lost. But the lights weren't like flashlights. Instead, they were more like laser beams, their light not diffusing as a flashlight's would but remaining in a tight one-inch column or tube. Each being held a different colored light—red, blue, green, and yellow.

It was utterly silent outside. Neither the beings nor their ship made a single sound, even though their footsteps should have been audible on the carpet of burned twigs and leaves. The old man had another dog, a mother with pups, that was chained up near the house because she tended to be very aggressive and territorial. This dog did not make a single sound either and remained in the doghouse with her puppies as the beings approached the house.

The old man's wood frame house had solar lights that ran across the front and around to the side, leading to an outhouse. Like most in this area, and on much of the Navajo Reservation, the old man did not have running water or indoor plumbing. He watched as the aliens followed the lights around the side of the house. At this point, he gathered his courage and went outside to confront the beings. He followed them around the side of the house to the back, where he tripped and fell. Of course, for a man in his eighties, a fall is no small thing. It took him several minutes to recover and get back to his feet. By this time, the beings were already back at the craft, which flashed all of its lights again and moved a few hundred yards to the south along the tree line before shooting at an angle into the sky like a colorful bullet.

At the end of his story, the old man shook his head and said that he had never experienced anything like this and didn't know why it had happened. He had lived through several wars and seen many changes in the world. He had worked in the railroad industry for his entire life, which often kept him outside under an empty sky. But this was the first time he had ever encountered something so strange and otherworldly.

As outlandish as his story seemed, I felt the truth of the old man's words. In fact, his story raised the hairs on the back of my neck. As a law enforcement officer, I am well trained in interrogation and know how to read body language and nonverbal cues and to detect nervousness or deceit. I detected nothing like this in our interview, and neither did Jon, who has extensive training in criminal investigation. The matter-of-fact, unembellished way the old man spoke and the consistency of the details of his story over multiple interviews convinced me he was telling the truth, at least as he believed it. In his unemotional, undramatic manner, he could have been describing a day of herding sheep or working at the railroad rather than a visitation from otherworldly beings. We had screened him for mental health or drinking issues, and there were no red flags. The old man was exactly what he seemed: an honest, clearheaded Navajo elder who had seen something extraordinary.

He was also completely uninterested in any publicity. As his story got around, a TV production company reached out and offered him a lot of money to share it on a show that was filming in the area. He steadfastly refused. He only wanted to share his story with the Rangers, as a way of archiving it. I suspect he felt that at the advanced age of eighty-five, he needed to get the story on record for posterity. As both Rangers and Navajos, Jon and I felt the weight of this encounter, standing in the presence of our elder, a man who was traditional in his beliefs and strong in his spirituality and culture. It moved us deeply.

After our initial interview, Jon and I walked the property to look for any signs of a craft or of the beings the old man saw. We found little tracks similar to a jack rabbit's but with a unique circular impression in the center of each track. We had never seen anything like it before. We also found a trail of markings in the area where the old man said the craft had been hovering. They were circular and equally spaced, several feet apart. The circular markings were approximately five inches in diameter. There were about twenty-five to thirty impressions that were observed leading away from the residence in a northwesterly angle in the direction where the old man had witnessed the object hovering. Whatever had made the marks went under brush and trees. It was difficult to detect these markings the farther they got from the house as the forest debris was too heavy. Jon and I couldn't figure out what might have made such impressions. I racked my brain, trying to figure out how they might be naturally occurring rather than paranormal in nature. But I couldn't imagine any ordinary scenario.

Instead, I had to fall back on the usual procedures and routines of investigation. We photographed all of the tracks. We also brought night vision goggles, thermal equipment, and infrared cameras to survey the area around the old man's home, as well as a Kestrel 4000 instrument to establish a baseline atmospheric reading—altitude, humidity, barometric pressure, dew point, windspeed, and the like. Nothing in particular stood out as unusual.

We next called in help from an environmental agency. Their technicians performed an environmental assessment to check for elevated levels of radiation. They reported that the radiation levels were indeed elevated around the old man's home, but that is not unusual for the

Navajo Nation, which is a hotspot for yellow ore, or uranium. This is, of course, the material used in the atomic bomb. Though the levels were elevated, the technicians did not consider them dangerous.

During investigations, law enforcement must sometimes call in civilian subject experts to help with cases. Jon and I knew of two organizations that had a history of UFO and extraterrestrial investigations. We felt it only made sense to reach out to them and take advantage of their superior knowledge of the subject matter. We first reached out to the Mutual UFO Network, or MUFON, which quickly dispatched a specialist from its STAR team in Phoenix. MUFON is an international organization that investigates UFO reports, alien abductions, and extraterrestrial contact. Its investigators are highly trained and often have law enforcement or technical backgrounds. Its STAR team has the most experienced members, a nationwide rapid response team that can quickly respond to high-value UFO investigations. MUFON is dedicated to UFO research and public education about extraterrestrials. I was surprised to find the specialist, Dominic Mancini, very down-to-earth and relatable, someone who was easy to talk to and work with.

We also reached out to Bigelow Aerospace, an organization known for conducting high-level work for the US government in UFO research and space engineering. Bigelow Aerospace was founded by billionaire Robert T. Bigelow and at the time was located in North Las Vegas, Nevada. They specialized in aeronautics and outer space technology, manufacturing expandable space station habitat modules. The company had a program called Bigelow Aerospace Advanced Space Studies that contracted in relation to the Advanced Aerospace Threat Identification Program that received $22 million dollars in funding from the federal government to study UAPs. Bigelow sent out two investigators with expensive equipment to help us. Unlike Dominic Mancini, they were very reserved and businesslike and seemed a bit more like the Men in Black you might be imagining. They arrived in a pickup truck and were dressed in clothing commonly used by military special operations team members: Battle Dress Uniform (BDU) pants and shirts. These are usually multi-pocketed pants and shirts, worn with tactical boots or chukkas. They stayed busy utilizing different types of specialized testing equipment. They clearly had a background in military special operations and were acutely focused on their mission objective. Jon and I avoided interrupting or disturbing them while they were busy using their equipment. They spoke rarely. They gave off strong Jason Bourne vibes, but I didn't mind. These guys had sophisticated, high-dollar equipment, whereas Jon and I had been used to buying our own tools and equipment and making do with what we had. I was glad to have their expertise and their equipment.

Both the MUFON representative and the guys sent out by Bigelow interviewed the elderly man, provided us with some guidance, and explored the area around his home, but neither team had any particular findings to share with us. We requested reports, which the organizations never provided. As they had received government funding, I suspect their information would be considered classified and was thus not available to us.

Even though these organizations did not share findings with us, I did feel that their interviews with the old man validated his story, as he did not change the details of his experience in the slightest, despite the interviews taking place over a period of several weeks. Some of his consistency, of course, is due to the Navajo culture being primarily an oral one, with stories being passed down over generations without alteration. But to me, it also spoke volumes about the old man's honesty and sincerity.

Through this case, Jon and I developed mutually beneficial relationships with MUFON and with the investigators who worked for Bigelow, both of which became a valuable connection for us in future cases and plugged us in to new opportunities relating to the paranormal. We would later assist MUFON with a field investigator training, or boot camp, in Phoenix to teach recruits how to conduct interviews, collect evidence, and deal with the general public. We also provided the organization with an opportunity to explore their interests in the Navajo Nation, which is, of course, a sovereign nation that they otherwise would not have access to.

There was one additional strange occurrence related to the case that still bothers me today. The man's dog, the little rez mutt that had run out to the sources of light, did return home after the aliens flew away, but it died a week after the events. Unfortunately, we weren't notified at the time and were not able to have a veterinarian examine the dog's remains. I couldn't help but wonder if the extraterrestrials had inadvertently injured it in some way in an attempt to defend themselves. Additionally, the old man's sister, who lived about a quarter of a mile away from him, had a litter of puppies go missing the following week after the UFO sighting. There were no signs of either animal predators or human thieves—the puppies just vanished. It was hard not to speculate about a connection between the UFO visitation and the puppies considering the context and timing. Perhaps it was similar to the sheep mutilations that I had witnessed as a rookie ranger or the abduction of cattle, which are not uncommon on the reservation.

This was only a small detail that didn't lead anywhere. The case as a whole, however, was a major turning point for Jon and me. Given the old man's credibility, we felt that his story validated some of the others we had heard on the reservation. We started getting a bigger picture of all these disparate cases and UFO sightings. It was clear to us that UFO activity was happening on the reservation, probably much more than we were even aware of.

We were also beginning to get a sense that many of our paranormal cases might be linked, including the ones involving Bigfoot. Perhaps, I thought, UFOs are interdimensional crafts. Rather than traveling through space in line of sight from one galaxy to ours as the crow flies, as with a human-made spacecraft, these beings are using dimensions as a means of getting from one place to another. They appear in Earth's atmosphere, but they are coming into the atmosphere from other galaxies. This made sense to me given the vast time and distance to be covered. The only logical means of travel would be via other dimensions, which also might account for the sudden appearance and disappearance of creatures like Bigfoot.

Despite bringing in all of the experts and spending a few nights outside the old man's home, we weren't able to witness additional UFO activity or find any other evidence. We did develop a strong relationship and sense of trust with the old man and his family, and even after his passing, about five years after his alien encounter, we stayed in contact with his relatives. The family continued to have UFO sightings over the years, witnessing lights, crafts, and other objects, and even glimpses of the little gray beings the old man had seen. We met with the old man's widow in 2022 and are planning to go back out to do follow-up interviews with other family members.

It's not hard to understand why UFO sightings are common on the reservation when you consider the vastness and remoteness of the landscape. There is little ambient light on the reservation, so any crafts coming into our atmosphere are highly visible. Still, I found myself wondering why these particular extraterrestrials might be attracted to the old man's area. Perhaps the radioactive material in the soil drew them. After all, one need only consider what use humans have made of uranium to imagine its potential value. It is capable of producing huge amounts of energy and may be a coveted material for extraterrestrials.

After this case, I would learn that the beings the old man saw are commonly known as "grays" among people who study extraterrestrial life. They are typically described as being three feet tall with a large head and large eyes, gray skin, a slit mouth, and no nose. They are always small and thin and have three to four long, slender fingers. Grays are probably the most common alien species described in extraterrestrial encounters throughout the world.

But there are many types of aliens that have been witnessed on Earth. There is another type nearly identical to the grays but much taller, closer to our height and size. There are also reptilian forms. A surprising kind of alien is one referred to as Nordics, historically seen frequently in Europe. These are human-like beings with pale, milky skin, blond hair, and sometimes very intense blue eyes. The universe is so vast that there could be infinite types of extraterrestrial life. Ufologist Dr. Steven Macon Greer, founder of the Center for the Study of Extraterrestrial Intelligence, has identified sixty to seventy distinct species of alien. I suspect that the extraterrestrial life-forms humans have encountered so far represent only a tiny portion of the potential alien life-forms that exist in the universe.

Along with their variations in appearance, there must be differing reasons for their visits to Earth, just as the non-Native people who visited North America came in different types of crafts and for different reasons. The concept of Star People, or people who come from the stars to Earth to help humans, is found throughout Native American tribes here in the United States and the First Nations tribes of Canada. There is a consensus among these tribes that extraterrestrial visitors have visited Earth to help us and guide us into the future.

Yet there are other reports of extraterrestrials that paint a much more horrific image of these visitors, such as the Mojave Incident of 1989, in which a couple was reportedly psychologically tortured by extraterrestrials in the Mojave Desert over a period of twenty-four hours. I feel that if you look at the history of humankind, there have been those individuals who help and protect their fellow man and there have been those who have no qualms about murdering and killing anyone and everyone. In the same way, in the vastness of our universe, you would find both extremes in extraterrestrials—those that would try to love and protect us and those that would try to kill us and eat us.

I started to wonder if the frequency of their visits is much higher than we are aware of because the aliens don't want to cause panic among humans. Maybe many people are unable to remember their contacts with extraterrestrials because it would be too traumatizing for them. Perhaps aliens choose a more covert form of contact or modify human memories.

The case of the old man and the UFO brought up more questions for me than it answered. But it was the first time I became absolutely certain that UFO activity on the reservation was real and that I began to seriously formulate a philosophy to explain the various paranormal phenomena my neighbors reported to the Rangers.

Then, a few years later, I had an extraterrestrial encounter of my own that turned all my theories into lived experience, transforming me from an objective investigator into someone who could truly understand what the old man felt when he saw the strange, otherworldly beings in his own front yard.

It was 2014, and I was working as a ranger sergeant. At the time there was nothing out of the ordinary occurring on the job or in my personal life, just work as usual and coming home to relax. I was single and living alone. Just as the old man had been entirely unprepared for his encounter with an alien, there was no foreshadowing of my own.

One night, I got in bed at the usual hour and read for a few minutes under the blue-hued overhead dimmer lights in my bedroom before switching them off with a remote. I lay down in the dark and got comfortable, expecting only a solid night's sleep before the next day's work.

At some point in the night, I came fully and instantly awake. It was like being thrown into the deep end of a very cold swimming pool. I blinked against a sudden harsh light.

Weird, why are the lights on? I wondered. I knew I didn't fall asleep reading under the overhead LED lights. I'd switched them off before going to sleep.

I tried to stretch out an arm for the remote, but nothing happened. I tried again. No movement.

I tried to move my feet, legs, head, hands, fingers. But I couldn't. I was paralyzed.

Panic spiked in my bloodstream, and I struggled desperately to move, to get out of bed. I strained with all of my being—every muscle, every ounce of my strength. I could feel the muscles in my back, arms, and legs contracting and straining, but nothing happened. I couldn't make my body work.

Trying to subdue the panic, I forced myself to think logically about what was happening. "Am I awake or dreaming?" I asked myself. I realized that my eyes were working normally, though I couldn't turn my head at all. I cast my eyes about the room as much as I was able, taking in the familiar surroundings of my bedroom: the guitars and baseball caps hanging on the wall, the mounted TV, the curtains on the windows, the shelves filled with books and CDs, a framed photo of my mother. I could even make out the crosshatch pattern on my sheets. It was all terribly clear. I wasn't dreaming.

But then I looked straight ahead toward the foot of the bed. A figure stood there in front of my closet, next to my dresser. Before I even fully understood what I was seeing, my body's fight or flight reaction kicked in—with a definite decision to fight. My law enforcement training had taught me that in a situation like this, such as a home invasion, you must initiate an instant and immediate response by attacking the assailant with as much force as possible to catch them off guard and gain an advantage over them and the overall situation. I knew this is what I ought to do. But I also knew that I couldn't—my body still wouldn't move. Not so much as a pinky finger was under my control.

Eyes wide, sweat pouring down my temples, I stared at the figure, which stared back at me, silent and unmoving. With no other recourse, no way to fight, I did the only thing I could: I studied it in all of its unbelievable detail. It was like the little green men I had read about and seen on TV, only it wasn't green. Its skin was a dull gray, the same color as the sculpting clay I had used to make pottery in junior high art class. It was solid in form—as real as you or me. I was sure, if I had been able to move, I could have reached out and touched it. Its head appeared larger than a human head, perhaps the size of a soccer ball but smaller than a basketball. It had the classic large, shiny black, wet-looking eyes that are commonly described by those who have witnessed grays. I thought its eyes looked more like goggles, reflecting the blue lights about the room. I couldn't perceive any ears, nose, or mouth, but it did have a noticeably small protruding chin. Extending downward from somewhat bony shoulders, its arms were very slender and appeared bony-looking too. Its neck and chest, what little I could see of them, were very thin. The chest was maybe just under twelve inches at the widest part. The being stood approximately four feet tall.

It soon became very clear to me that, whatever this entity was, either it hadn't bathed in a while or had a natural stink like nothing I'd encountered. There was an extremely sickening, putrid, petroleum-like stench pervading the room. It reminded me more than anything of the air surrounding oil drilling fields, combined with the odor of something dead or decaying. It was extremely nauseating, and I felt like I would vomit.

For a long, seemingly endless time, the alien stood there silently watching, staring, but not moving and not saying or doing anything. I realized I was not hearing anything either; the room was completely silent. There were none of the usual familiar sounds, like cars and trucks on the interstate, or the trains running back and forth on the Santa Fe railroad, or the whir of my bedroom fan. I couldn't make out even the faintest of sounds, apart from my own jagged breathing and pounding heartbeat. It was like having earplugs in, almost like the quiet of being in a sensory deprivation chamber. No sound could reach me, except what I myself made.

The terror of it all was nearly unbearable—the feeling of being restrained, out of my own control; the strange, otherworldly being standing there watching; the silence pressing in on me. I began to hyperventilate. My mind flashed through one bad thought after another: *Is this it? Am I going to die? Lying here in my own bed?* It certainly wasn't the death I'd imagined for myself as a law enforcement officer. I tried to fight those despairing thoughts off, but they were all-consuming. I wasn't sure how much longer I could remain conscious.

Then, without warning, the paralysis left me, like a light switch being flipped. All my muscles must have been straining to jump up out of the bed because when the paralysis stopped, it was almost like being launched off a gymnast's springboard. I snapped forward and sprung to my feet, already in a fighting stance, my fists clenched. I was ready to pounce on this thing, but it was gone. The entity had vanished.

Without stopping to think, I retrieved my handgun from its locked box, and using the tactical utility light mounted on it, began searching under the bed, in the closet, and anywhere else this thing could have been hiding. But there was nothing in my room. I flipped on the main light switch and continued a more thorough tactical room clearing and search throughout the house. I yanked open doors and pushed objects out of the way, single-minded in my search. I checked the bedroom window and the other windows throughout the house to see if they were open or had been tampered with. Nothing—they were all secure, as were the doors. The entity that had been in my bedroom only moments before was undeniably gone now.

As I came down off the adrenaline high and the shock, I slumped down into a recliner in the living room. But my brain was still racing to try to figure out what the hell had just happened. Did it really happen? I knew without a doubt that it had. I still had a nasty taste in my mouth from the putrid, sickening smell that had permeated my entire bedroom just minutes earlier. Rubbing my eyes, I looked at the clock. It was five a.m.

I got up and went back to my bedroom and stood there looking about the room where this strange, terrifying experience had played out. Everything looked normal, except a little messier than usual from my search. Nothing had changed, and yet everything had changed. The previous safety and sanctity of my bedroom had been breached— the place I retreated to for comfort when tired from work or when I wasn't feeling well, the place I turned to when I simply wanted to lie down and clear my thoughts to heal myself mentally, spiritually, and physically from the sometimes-damaging effects of life. All of that had been violated, and I knew I wouldn't recover from it quickly. I am a trained law enforcement officer who deals with upsetting events all the time. If the experience was frightening for me, I cannot imagine how terrifying it would be for the average person.

Still half convinced the being must be lurking somewhere, I checked under the bed and in the closet again before finally securing my handgun. I was about to get back in bed and try to sleep when I realized something wasn't right with my T-shirt. It felt strange against my chest and too tight, like it was choking me. The tag stuck up, scratching against my neck. On closer inspection, I discovered it was inside out and backward. Then I noticed my pajama bottoms were also inside out and backward. "What the hell?" I murmured to myself.

Unsettled once more, I looked around the room to see if there was any physical evidence of my recent visitor but wasn't able to detect anything. There was no discoloration or odor. The odor that had been extremely off-putting earlier was now gone, like it had never occurred. I checked the carpeting where the entity had been standing. Nothing. Then I marked and took measurements along the closet door from memory, determining that the alien measured four feet, two inches in height—two inches taller than my dresser. My bed at the time was a common box spring, on a metal frame with mattress or spring coils, which when measured was thirty inches or two feet, six inches in height. This left about twenty inches of the entity that had been visible to the top of its head. Of course, my view was restricted due to my inability to move my head, neck, or body, but my head was on a pillow, which elevated my view some. Taking all of this into account, I was satisfied that my memory squared with the physical dimensions of the room and my place in it.

Apart from these measurements, the only evidence I had of the visitation was my own memory and the disarrangement of my pajamas—a fact with implications I was not sure I wanted to understand.

I fixed my pajamas and laid back down on the bed thinking about the strange event. I was already completely exhausted even though I was used to waking very early and had only been up for a short time. What had happened to me? How long had the alien been in my bedroom? What had it done? Had I lost time, or did the entire episode take only seconds?

As terrifying as the episode had been, my gut feeling told me that whatever this thing was, whatever it might have done, it hadn't intended me any harm. I may have been wrong, but that was the overall feeling I had—not that I had been purposefully harmed or that the being had wished me ill. The terror it had caused me seemed unintentional, though I couldn't have said why. I had the sense that it hadn't meant for me to wake up, that I had caught the tail end of a visitation I wasn't meant to experience or remember.

The other thing I pondered was why was there no communication from the being. Why did this entity not communicate anything, or make any sounds or gestures during the time I saw it? What if the gut feeling that I had was, in fact, a form of communication from this thing? Maybe it wanted me to know that it didn't wish me harm and had communicated that to me in another way, apart from speech or gesture. Maybe that's why, despite the violation of my bedroom and possibly even my person, I didn't feel that it had intentionally wronged me.

As I lay there, my mind playing over the minute details of the incident, my eyes gradually grew heavy and closed. The next thing I knew, I rolled over and looked at my alarm clock. It was almost nine a.m. Bright daylight seeped through my closed curtains.

I understand that those in the mental health and medical fields would say that I experienced sleep paralysis, the feeling of being conscious and unable to move. I do know that this condition occurs between stages of sleep—where, in the moments between wakefulness and sleep, for a brief moment you can't move or speak. I have talked with others who have experienced sleep paralysis and their accompanying hallucinations, night terrors, and the like. But I have also spoken with those whose experiences were more like my own, who felt sure that what had happened was entirely real. I don't see why both experiences cannot be possible and valid.

But I know that mere sleep paralysis is not what I experienced. I did not simply imagine it or hallucinate it. All of my senses were working quite well throughout the event. I was thinking logically and systematically, even in the midst of my terror. I was in my mid-forties at the time, knew I had not been drinking or using drugs, and that I had no underlying psychological or medical issues that might explain it. I had had enough life experiences by that time to determine if I was in a state of being awake, dreaming, or hallucinating. I was one hundred percent confident that I had witnessed an extraterrestrial, though of course I couldn't say why it had happened—or even *what* had happened.

It would be simple enough to slap a label like sleep paralysis on an encounter that I can't fully understand or explain. But this is the easy way out, a Western response to the things that frighten or confuse us. Just because I cannot fully explain the event doesn't make me think it wasn't real. While, as an investigator, I would prefer to always have evidence and answers, my experiences with the paranormal have taught me to coexist with mystery when I must.

Even so, I didn't tell anyone about the experience for a long time. I think I was still in shock that it had happened. I suppose I also felt the weight of the taboos around these issues in a way I hadn't experienced before. I kept asking myself if I had somehow caused this encounter to occur. I wondered if by investigating so many paranormal cases, I had inadvertently opened myself up to larger forces. There was also a lingering feeling of violation and trauma.

I can only compare what I went through to the experience of being carjacked at gunpoint. Imagine, one minute it's a bright, sunny day, blue skies all around, and you're driving to work as you have done a million times before. You're enjoying a nice, hot cup of Starbucks or Dutch Bros, maybe singing along to your favorite song on the car radio. Then you pull up to the stoplight, and all of a sudden some masked figure dressed in black with menacing eyes full of hate is shoving the barrel of a very large handgun against your nose, shouting expletives at you, and threatening to blow your head off if you don't get out of the car. Automatically, you thrust your hands into the air and willingly surrender your automobile in trade for your life. The experience leaves you mentally, physically, spiritually broken and violated. You stand there shaking, embarrassed, alone, eyes wide, traumatized, with your brain trying to contemplate what has just happened, questioning why your Higher Power allowed this to happen to you. This is exactly what it felt like for me to encounter the alien species known as a gray.

In those few minutes I'd been pinned to my bed, unable to move or speak or defend myself in any way, I had been as helpless as a child. It was difficult to speak with anyone about those kinds of feelings, and I did not like to be reminded of the vulnerability of those moments. It was only years later, when my partner Jon told me about a personal experience he had had with extraterrestrial life, that I felt safe enough to share my story.

I only share it now publicly so that others will know they aren't alone if they have had a similar experience. They aren't crazy, delusional, or misguided. I think that hearing the testimony of the elderly Navajo man in Ganado, a person for whom I felt respect and esteem, in some ways prepared me for having my own experience with an extraterrestrial. Because of his simple witness, I did not doubt myself or the experience. I hope that in the same way, my testimony here will provide a steadying hand to anyone who may need it.

CHAPTER 8

The Satan Butte Phenomena
2010

THE NEW RELATIONSHIP WITH THE MUTUAL UFO NETWORK that Jon and I established during the Old Man case proved useful as they brought our next big UFO-related case to us. The investigator we worked with on the Old Man case, Dominic Mancini, emailed Jon and me to let us know about a case on the Navajo Reservation that had been reported to MUFON.

I was glad to work with Dominic again. He is one of the most likeable people I've met during my work as a Navajo Ranger. He is a tall, slim man with a background in law enforcement. For his day job, Dominic worked as an investigator at a casino on the Fort McDowell Yavapai or We-Ko-Pa Reservation in Fountain Hills near Scottsdale, Arizona. We had enjoyed working with him on the previous case, and the new investigation he looped us into would prove to be just as fascinating.

Hoss Lors, a white, non-Native ESL teacher who lived on the reservation with his Navajo wife, had reported a UFO sighting to MUFON, along with other paranormal activity that coincided with the UFO sighting.

It all started with lights in the sky.

Hoss lived in a mobile home on a small farm in Greasewood, Arizona, about a mile to the east of the mesa known as Satan Butte. The desert-like area he lived in was wide open for miles around, with very few trees except near the arroyos. Cottonwood trees grew along the dry creek bottoms, and sagebrush was very prevalent throughout the area. There was little else there besides long stretches of dusty highway. As the only piece of elevated land in the area, Satan Butte inevitably drew the eye, standing stark and clear against an open sky.

Satan Butte has a long and storied reputation among Navajos. One legend says that there is a giant serpent that lives inside the butte and comes out from a hole at the top. This made the butte a restricted area for Navajos in the past—a time long before the Long Walk. If your cattle strayed onto the butte, you didn't go retrieve them. Either they returned on their own, or you considered them lost. Navajos refused to venture onto the mesa. This serpent is likely the reason the mesa is called Satan Butte, harkening, of course, to the serpent in the Garden of Eden in the Bible's Book of Genesis.

But it wasn't the mesa that drew Hoss's eye—it was something in the air above it.

One night near dusk, when Hoss went outside to feed the horses, as he did every night, he noticed a strange light hovering above Satan Butte, and he couldn't figure out what it was. A few nights later, he saw it again. He described it as a large UFO ship shaped like a spade, with red lights going across and several tendrils of light extending from it. The lights looked a bit like teardrops moving toward the earth. He wondered if these were smaller ships exiting the UFO craft. He reported that the object not only flew above and around Satan Butte but that it also flew *into* the mesa, as if passing through solid rock. Its movement seemed very purposeful and intentional.

A week later, Hoss saw the UFO again, and from then on, he saw the lights in the sky over Satan Butte repeatedly. He reported the sightings to his wife, who didn't believe him—at least not at first. Later on, she would witness the lights with her own eyes. But at the time, she must have thought he was exaggerating and dismissed his claims. Undeterred, Hoss drove into Flagstaff and bought a high-quality digital camera, determined to capture pictures of the UFO. His resulting photos show an object with blurred trails of light extending from it.

MUFON's technical experts analyzed Hoss's photos to determine whether they had been faked. Dominic assured us that the organization was positive that the photos had not been altered or modified in any way. Additionally, the photos included visual references from around Hoss's property to demonstrate the locations from which the photos were taken. In one, you can see the outline of the open back door of his mobile home, as well as a propane tank in the yard. It was clear to Dominic and to us that Hoss was seeing something out of the ordinary.

But it turned out that Hoss's unusual sightings were not limited to lights in the sky. He came into much, much closer contact with the paranormal—only not in the form of extraterrestrials.

One day Hoss was working in the garage when a mangy, scraggly stray dog came into the yard. It looked very sick and had signs of being infected with rabies. Hoss's other dogs were afraid and wouldn't go near it, so he put the dogs in the house and went back outside to deal with the stray. Hoss realized he would have to put the creature out of its misery. Calling animal control to deal with stray dogs simply wasn't—and still isn't—an option on the Navajo Reservation. The reservation is huge, and most people are poor. The service is needed, but for many communities there is simply not enough funding to create and maintain an animal control department. This has resulted in very large stray and feral dog populations, which can sometimes be extremely dangerous. In 2021, a thirteen-year-old girl in my own family, Lyssa Rose, was attacked and killed by a pack of dogs in broad daylight in Fort Defiance, Arizona. Many people from Europe and other places come to the Navajo Reservation and are shocked and traumatized to see the conditions many stray dogs are in. But it's simply an unfortunate part of the Navajo reality.

So, what Hoss did next was both self-protective and intended as a mercy for the sick dog that had wandered into his yard. He grabbed a two-by-four and clubbed the dog on the head, killing it. As he did so, a plume of what he thought was dust or dirt wafted up from the dog. He made sure the dog was dead and then covered it with a scrap of material from the garage before going inside to tell his wife that he was going to take the dog's body away to get rid of it.

But when Hoss came back outside, the rabid dog was gone, along with the material he had used to cover it. Hoss was certain that the dog had been dead, and there were no tracks in the dirt to show that it had run off. He couldn't find any sign of the creature.

Within hours, Hoss became very, very sick. He was curled up in bed with an illness akin to a stomach virus, only far worse. As he became sicker and more disoriented, his wife, who was traditional in her beliefs, wanted to take him to a medicine man. But Hoss refused. At that point, he did not believe in Navajo medicine. But he eventually became so sick that his wife saw no other choice. She felt that a Western doctor would not be able to deal with what ailed her husband, which she firmly believed to be witchcraft. She got a friend to help put him in the car and drove him straight to the medicine man. The medicine man performed a healing ritual using bitter herbs. This is a common practice of both medicine men and laypeople on the Navajo Reservation. I use bitter medicine, or bitter herb, and other Navajo medicine when I have been attacked by someone using witchcraft. These medicines are sacred to the Navajo people, so though I am sure readers would like more details about this ritual, I do not feel it is appropriate to share specific details. To do so could potentially negate the use of these powerful tools.

After the medicine man's treatment, Hoss recovered almost instantly, like flipping a switch. The medicine man explained that what Hoss had thought was a rabid dog was, in fact, a skinwalker, and that the dust that had plumed up from its fur when he struck it was corpse dust, a type of poison used in witchcraft. It is made from the ashes of a burned human corpse. When Hoss breathed it in, the curse took hold.

Only a few weeks later, Hoss saw two more skinwalkers. These appeared in a similar guise to werewolves, or wolf-men, with red eyes. He got out his pistol and tried to shoot at them, but the gun wouldn't fire, despite being fully loaded. It just made a *click-click-click* sound. But the threat of the gun was apparently enough to scare them off, and the skinwalkers fled. Hoss ran after them but didn't catch them. When he tried to fire the pistol the next day, it worked fine. This didn't surprise me as I'd heard several stories from others where guns didn't work on skinwalkers. The individuals responsible for the skinwalkers are performing black witchcraft that can and does result in magical supernatural acts, such as making a firearm that is in good working condition and properly maintained unable to fire in a specific moment and context—though later, the gun will function normally. I'm aware of several instances where individuals I know attempted to shoot a skinwalker and the gun failed to fire. One individual is a firearms expert, who was a former Navajo Police officer.

Within a few days of the second skinwalker incident, something began bothering Hoss's horses. The horses were blowing and snorting, and they were all huddled up in one corner of the corral. Hoss expected to find a predator troubling the horses, but instead a cylindrical, vertical object hung in the air near the corral. The horses were desperately try-ing to get away from it. The object was approximately eight feet tall, and some kind of haze or mist hung around it. Puzzled and alarmed, Hoss grabbed a pellet gun and shot it. He heard the bullet ping off the metal, then instantaneously, the object shot toward a neighbor's home, went around the house, and disappeared.

This was quite a lot of paranormal activity for one person to bear, so it wasn't surprising that Hoss reached out to MUFON for help. On a clear, bright day, Jon and I drove out to the base of Satan Butte to meet with him.

When you arrive in the area of Satan Butte on Navajo Route 15, the landscape is wide open. You can literally see from horizon to horizon, approximately fifteen miles in any direction, and there is very little in the way of trees or foliage to obstruct your view. From the highway there is a rough mile and a half off-road drive that is best attempted in a four-wheel-drive SUV or truck. If you want to go up onto the butte, you must hike up a narrow canyon on foot. But we weren't climbing that day.

We met Hoss at the base of the butte rather than at his home for two reasons. First of all, the focus of the activity he was witnessing at the time was at Satan Butte. Second, I think he was very untrusting of government representatives and didn't want us near his home. We were fine with this arrangement and didn't demand to meet at his residence. A lot of these paranormal cases required additional consideration of what the victim was experiencing and the trauma of what this person had just gone through. Despite our willingness to adapt to his needs, I think Jon and I still put him on guard when we arrived, each of us in identical metallic gray trucks with several antennae, plus our matching uniforms. We must have looked like the might of the government falling upon him—like Men in Black from Area 51. He admitted later that he had suspected we were Feds.

But his suspicion didn't last long. When we talked to him, we did not speak with that "us versus them" attitude that many law enforcement officers or police tend to use. To be a good investigator you must be able to build rapport and trust with the people you are working with. Jon and I were good at this. We did our best to get to his level, and he soon realized we were there to help and warmed up to us. Later on, he did invite us to investigate around his residence, but there were no obvious paranormal events happening at the time.

Hoss was stocky in build and had a loud, clear voice, which he used freely. It was immediately clear to me that he was intense and had a big personality, but he didn't seem to be lying about his experiences. He struck me as serious, religious, and truthful. I felt that he was sincere in his claims. He truly had experienced something out of the ordinary and was very concerned that he or his wife could have been harmed or even killed by the phenomena on their property. Jon and I both felt his case was well worth looking into.

Personally, I felt a deep empathy for him because I remembered what it was like to encounter a skinwalker, and even after all the years that had passed, the emotions of that experience still felt raw to me. Seeing that skinwalker was like seeing the devil himself—an unforgettable, scarring experience. Whenever something similar arises, it touches on those feelings and nerves that I know will never fully heal or recover. Hoss's case brought up the memories and sensations of that experience in an incredibly powerful way, making me feel even more determined to help him if we could. I knew that whether we were able to find any evidence in his case or not, we would at least be able to make him feel heard and make sure he was as safe as possible.

In the course of his story, it came out that the UFO sighting wasn't actually when everything started. There had been one even stranger event that kick-started Hoss's entire series of paranormal sightings. One day, out near the corral, Hoss heard a Navajo song coming from an unseen location. It was sung in the Navajo language without accompanying instruments and seemed fast in tempo. It sounded as if it were coming from the very ground beneath his feet. He went inside and got his wife, who was fluent in Navajo, to listen and interpret. The song soon evolved into a chant. His wife said that it was a curse against him and their land and property. Hoss became angry at this news and started swearing loudly at whoever was doing this.

After the curse from invisible music came the skinwalkers and the UFOs. After that came Hoss's illness.

There did not seem to be any particular individuals who wished Hoss harm. He hadn't fought with anyone or done anything to make someone send skinwalkers after him, at least not that he was aware of. But the living were not the only people worth considering in this case. After all, in the Navajo Nation, you are always walking on ruins. You are always walking on land that once belonged to someone else, where Native people have lived for thousands of years. As good and well-meaning of a person as he was, Hoss was still a white, non-Native man, on the reservation to teach English to Navajo children, married to a Navajo woman. There were almost no other white people in this area. Given Hoss's big and colorful personality, in addition to his large and imposing physique, he would have stood out even more, as Navajos, especially older ones, tended to be much more reserved and subdued in nature; in contrast, Hoss liked to make small talk and joke around.

He had been living in Greasewood for only a year when all of the paranormal activity began. Perhaps the spirits who resided in that place resented his presence and actions on their ancestral lands. Certainly, the Navajos who endured the Long Walk or lived during the turmoil and oppression of the 1800s or the parents who had their children stolen and put into boarding schools would not look positively on such a person. Hoss's job teaching English and Western values to Navajo children would be deeply offensive and threatening to some of these individuals, who fought tooth and nail to keep Western education out of the reservation. In fact, an individual known as Black Horse once tried

to kill a government agent who was recruiting—or perhaps capturing—
Navajo students for the school at Fort Defiance. The man was being es-
corted by Chief Chee Dodge, who at the time was a young man and not
yet president. No one died, but this incident was indicative of the anger
and distrust many Navajos felt for Western education. It isn't hard to
imagine that Hoss's very presence on the reservation might be offensive
to the spirits of that place. Over the years of paranormal investigation,
I have learned that some spirits do not even realize their bodies have
passed on. Navajos from the past may have never encountered a white
man or have had only negative experiences with white people, so they
could see non-Navajos as strange or foreign to their lands, and view
Hoss as a genuine trespasser.

Of course, this is only conjecture. Perhaps he simply had the bad
luck to move to a paranormal hotspot. He settled down in the middle of a vortex of negative energies, a cauldron of historical turmoil.
There is no way to know what events might have occurred on that piece
of land—the cultures that were practiced there and conflicts they endured. Perhaps there was fighting, chaos, death. Perhaps the energy
from those times is still retained in the very soil and air of the place, and
Hoss possessed the kind of sensitivity to those energies that allowed
them to make themselves known and felt. Maybe something in his nature made him especially vulnerable.

Certainly, I felt those energies as I walked the land during this case
and then again later on, when I hiked up Satan Butte with Jon Dover
and Robert Bigelow's investigators. Both times, my sixth sense went
off like an alarm, letting me know that something wasn't right. Jon, the
investigators, and I hiked several hundred feet to the top of the butte
and spent the better part of a day up there. It was vast, open terrain
and very eerie. Standing on the top of the butte is like standing on the
moon. There are few, if any, bushes, trees, or other foliage and there are
zero structures on the top and no man-made structures visible in any

direction. So, one has the sense of being all alone on Earth, which is a strange, creepy, and downright unnerving feeling. Yet at the same time, I had a very strong sensation that I was being watched. When I am in the presence of ghosts, spirits, foreign entities, or something demonic, I experience a sharp pain above my temple. This pain was very strong here, so I knew danger was close.

We used the Bigelow team's sophisticated electronics and took readings of our own. I took electromagnetic frequency, or EMF, readings using a Trifield meter. An EMF meter, or Gauss meter, has been established as a viable tool to be used in various types of paranormal investigation. In the case of hauntings, some scientists theorize that an electromagnetic field is present in the conscious mind of a living person, and in many instances does not simply disappear upon one's death. Albert Einstein is often quoted as saying, "Energy cannot be created or destroyed; it can only be changed from one form to another," a restatement of the first law of thermodynamics. If a human brain functions by utilizing neurons, which are the electrical component for the brain's electrical process intertwined with a chemical process for endless bodily functions and operations, maybe it is still present after death and can, in some cases, still be detected. Our EMF meter picked up very high, unusual frequencies there, indicating that there was indeed spirit activity on the butte.

Bigelow's guys were very secretive about the equipment they were using. I think it goes back to their CIA-like compartmentalization methods. They did not offer up any information about their equipment, and I did not ask. We also looked for overt signs of something landing or making contact with the ground. We did not find any such evidence. Bigelow's men were once again nearly silent. If they found anything, they chose not to share it.

However, on a third visit, I heard voices as I began the climb up the mesa, as well as whistling. Navajos do not whistle, especially at night, as whistling is associated with witchcraft and skinwalkers. Witches use a bone whistle in their cursing. Therefore, the sounds I heard sent goose bumps trailing across my skin. I saw things moving in my peripheral vision, but when I turned my head, there was nothing there. But my sixth sense was fully in play, and my gut instincts were heightened. This was not a place to relax or let down your guard.

I felt intensely that the energies of that place did not want us there. High, hurricane-like winds came up suddenly, as if trying to blow us and our equipment right off the mesa. We had to hold tight to our equipment to keep it from being blown away. Given the forbidding nature of Satan Butte and the stories Navajos have told about it for generations, it is not impossible that black magic was once performed there, or even human sacrifices. We can make educated guesses about previous cultures who occupied the region, but we simply cannot know all that went on at such a location. The Navajo legend of the snake that lived inside the butte may even hint at something darker considering its relationship to the biblical snake of the Garden of Eden, as well as Navajos' particularly strong revulsion toward snakes that is practically a taboo. Perhaps there was a very real and serious reason that the ancestors wished to warn Navajos away from Satan Butte.

Interestingly, the Satan Butte case took place only about a hundred miles from the location of the Old Man case, as the crow flies. The locations are both also on the same longitude as Skinwalker Ranch in Utah, a place that is now famous for its paranormal and UFO activity. Skinwalker Ranch borders the Uintah and Ouray Indian Reservation. There have been paranormal and UFO phenomena reported there for decades, including skinwalkers, UFOs, orbs, cattle mutilations, and strange magnetic fields. These events have been highly publicized on the reality TV series *The Secret of Skinwalker Ranch*.

This constellation of hotspots is what many would consider a *ley line*, an invisible line connecting locations where magic or paranormal phenomena are particularly strong. Some even think we can cross from the physical world to other dimensions at such places. There are naturally occurring places like this that act as gateways, such as Sedona, Arizona, a well-known hotspot for high strangeness, vortexes, UFOs, paranormal activity, unusual energies, and the appearance of otherworldly entities.

Sedona possesses an intoxicating scenic beauty, featuring magnificent red rock sandstone formations off in the distance, set among the green-forested hills, mesas, and mountains. Sedona also has an unmistakable relaxed and laid-back vibe or positive energy in the air that is almost palpable. It is known as a hippie or artist commune and a haven of Native American peoples. But it is also a place of vortexes, or portals—places that are prone to focused non-electric or non-magnetic energy. There are many places like this in and around Sedona, including Bell Rock, Cathedral Rock, Airport Mesa, Red Rock Crossing, and Boynton Canyon. The vortexes are seen by many as places where one can access strong positive energy for meditation, healing, prayer, and balancing of Chakras. Jon Dover and I have visited Sedona many times, and on each of our visits, there was always a noticeable and unique sense of connection to the land, environment, and people there.

Along with the vortexes, Sedona can be considered a paranormal hotspot due to its association with the infamous Bradshaw Ranch, which is located about twelve miles outside of Sedona. It was once owned by movie stuntman Bob Bradshaw in the 1960s. It was used as a set and backdrop for filming commercials and movie productions, and also offered horseback riding, wagon rides, dining, and dancing. During the time Bradshaw and his wife were living there, they experienced various strange phenomena in and around the area, very similar to that of the more well-known Skinwalker Ranch. Sightings at Bradshaw Ranch included UFOs, orbs, Bigfoot-like creatures, portals, Grey aliens and other extraterrestrial beings, military helicopters, and official-looking men dressed in black—all the usual paranormal hotspot fare. It was later purchased by the US government for several million dollars and fenced off.

Sedona is an excellent example of a naturally occurring paranormal hotspot. However, these supernatural gateways can also be human-made, created by turmoil and violence on a mass scale, such as Gettysburg, Pennsylvania. Gettysburg is one of—if not *the*—most actively haunted paranormal hotspots, not only in the United States but around the world. The lands in and around Gettysburg are forever stained with the blood, bodies, and souls of 51,000 American soldiers, both Confederate and Union, who were either killed, wounded, or ended up missing—the largest number of casualties of the entire war. Five thousand horses also died on that field. These individuals fought for or against the cause of slavery between Wednesday, July 1 through Friday, July 3, 1863, in what is called the bloodiest battle of the Civil War. The amount of human carnage and trauma that occurred at that one location is so monumental it is nearly impossible for the human mind to comprehend—row after row after row of American fathers, grandfathers, sons, brothers, uncles, and cousins, all of whom lost their lives on America's own soil in arguably the darkest *three days* of Civil War history.

Today, Gettysburg is known as a site of significant paranormal activity, particularly hauntings by Civil War soldiers. Because of the extreme violence of the soldiers' deaths, visitors to this landmark have experienced haunting activity of at least two different types: One is known as a *residual haunting*, where the activity is like that of a recording that is looped and being played back over and over and essentially never changing. And the second type is classified as an *intelligent haunting*, or sometimes referred to as an *active haunting*, where a spirit or ghost actively responds or interacts with a living person in real time.

Paranormal hotspots like these are marked by the worst parts of humanity: our egos, pride, greed, lust, envy, gluttony, and wrath. They are stained with our blood, charged with our violence, brimming over with our desperation and pain. They are volatile places where volatile paranormal activity is present.

Perhaps Hoss's property was just such a place.

Jon and I, as well as the representatives from MUFON, did everything we could to help Hoss, and he appreciated how quickly we were able to mobilize. We did not find any evidence of witchcraft ourselves, such as bundles of sticks or signs of skinwalkers. Nor did we witness any UFO activity, though I had no trouble believing there was plenty to be had given the extremely strange and intense energies of the place.

I wish I could say that things ended happily for Hoss Lors, but unfortunately that is not the case. Both he and his wife experienced significant illness while living on the land. Hoss was traumatized by his experiences and felt that he no longer belonged. He moved off the reservation, which is perhaps what the spirits who tormented him had wished for all along.

After years of encountering and learning about paranormal hotspots, especially the ones in the United States that resulted from extreme violence, I have come to feel strongly about what we should learn from them. Places like these are an invitation for us to examine our hearts and attitudes, both as individuals and as societies. I think my own country in particular needs to look to these hotspots to understand and acknowledge our violent history, the harm done to Native Americans, African Americans, immigrants, women, the elderly, and those with disabilities. We also need to look at the harm we have done to one another in our stubborn pride and refusal to cooperate. Just as the separation of men and women in the Navajo creation story gave birth to violent and terrifying monsters, so too have we created haunted, tormented places through our division and strife.

I think we could all benefit from a trip to Gettysburg—to take the time to walk among the endless fields that stretch as far as the eye can see, littered with an unthinkable number of American graves; to feel their spirits and energy, their loss, their sadness, their regret and their pain; and to examine what is in our own hearts and consider how we can live with *hózhó*, or harmony and balance. I think in doing so, the world would be a much safer, more enjoyable, and overall better place to live, raise our children, and care for the sick and elderly. We should view paranormal hotspots as reminders of the pain we can inflict and how long-lasting the effects of violence can be—lest in our pride and selfishness we allow more places like Gettysburg to be created.

THE COMING OF DEATH

Toward evening on the first day of First Man and First Woman's life in the Fourth World, the Shining World, one of the twins called Nádleeh, who was neither Male nor Female, suddenly stopped breathing and lay very still. The People were frightened by this and did not know what to do. They left her alone and went away.

The next day, when they returned to find her, she was gone. Coyote First Angry and some of the People went to look for her. One of the Men had the idea to look down through the reed into the Third World from which they had emerged the day before. To his surprise, there sat Nádleeh combing her hair by the riverside. He called over to his friend, who looked down and saw Nádleeh too. They asked Coyote First Angry what to do.

Coyote threw a black stone into Black Water Lake. He said that if it floated to the surface, then Nádleeh would return to them. But if it sank, Nádleeh would be dead and remain in the Third World. The People agreed to this. Of course, the stone sank, just as Coyote First Angry knew that it would. Thus, death entered the World.

Soon, the two Men who had looked down through the reed at Nádleeh also stopped breathing, lay still, and died. This is how the People learned that it is dangerous to look at the dead or to see a ghost.

The People were angry at Coyote First Angry for bringing death into the world. But he explained to them that without death, the Shining World would be too full of People; the sick and infirm would be stuck in bodies that hurt them; and there would not be enough food and supplies for the new Children who would be born.

The People, though grieved by the loss of Nádleeh and the two Men who had looked at Nádleeh through the reed, saw the wisdom of Coyote First Angry's words and accepted the role that death plays in the World.

CHAPTER 9

The Window Rock Haunting

2010

TRADITIONAL NAVAJOS DO NOT SPEAK THE NAMES OF THE dead at night. They don't go wandering around after dark. They certainly don't want anything to do with haunted locations.

In Navajo culture, nighttime belongs to the spirits, and it is wise to stay safe in your home with the door locked. You wake before sunrise, say your prayers, complete your work, and eat your nightly meal before the sun sets. Nothing good wanders around at night, so neither do you. Nighttime is when witches do their work and skinwalkers prowl. Spirits move freely in the darkness, waiting for someone to invite them in. Words have power and names are precious; to speak freely and idly of the dead after dark is to put yourself in their power.

Navajos avoid meddling with the supernatural at all costs, no matter what time of day. That is work for medicine men, not ordinary people. The taboo against engaging with spirits is strong, and anything to do with the dead is treated with extreme caution. The Emergence story teaches that looking at a dead body or meddling with the spirit world can lead to sickness and death, as it did for the men who looked through the reed into the Third World to see Nádleeh combing her hair by the riverside. In addition to traditional Navajo beliefs about death, nighttime, and spirits, Christian beliefs about demons and evil also permeate the reservation. Christian religion spread like wildfire through the Navajo homelands following the Long Walk, with the reservation divided up among different denominations: Catholics, Baptists, Mormons, and others. Western beliefs about the afterlife, demons, and evil blended with traditional beliefs, strengthening the taboos.

Thus, there are few on the Navajo reservation who would do what I was about to do.

It was 8:30 on a cool evening in late November 2010 when I pulled up to the building, a two-story sandstone giant that had been built in the 1930s. I studied the building, already imagining what strange presences might lurk inside. It was a familiar office building in Window Rock, Arizona, one I'd seen many times before. It had served several purposes over the decades: movie theater, playhouse, library, mundane office building, occasionally even a makeshift morgue during times of mass pandemics. Now it was a government office building.

My chief had received a call from the director of the government program currently using the building as an office space. She said that nearly all of her employees—ten to fifteen individuals—had experienced paranormal phenomena that were deeply disruptive and making it difficult for everyone to do their jobs. After meeting with the director and speaking with her employees, I knew this case was well worth looking into. The employees had heard disembodied voices, felt unseen hands touch them, saw office supplies move across the room, and witnessed many other strange incidents. One woman who served in the administrative services department of the organization received several untraceable phone calls at her desk every day, during which the caller remained silent or breathed into the phone. She had contacted both the police and the phone company, and neither could figure out where the calls were coming from. She had been documenting each one in a spiral notebook, and there were pages and pages of entries.

I, of course, considered the possibility that the woman simply had a stalker, despite the phone company's inability to trace the calls. I took a detailed account of her personal life. She said there was a particular person in her life that she knew wished her harm and that she suspected had been using witchcraft against her. After hearing this, I had to consider that witchcraft might be involved in what was going on in the office building, which made the case much more serious.

I knew that when the building was remodeled and commissioned for use as a government office, a medicine man and representatives from other religious groups had blessed it and performed prayers before the building opened for use. However, a close friend of mine who is a medicine man says that you can never really get rid of spiritual energy—you can only temporarily appease it. Perhaps the witchcraft used against the woman reactivated what was already there in the building, I thought.

I met with my chief and with Jon, though he wouldn't be part of the case for personal reasons. I talked over the details with them and presented my plan, which Chief approved. I had determined to spend two evenings in the building after dark. I chose the Friday and Saturday of a tribal holiday weekend near Thanksgiving to ensure that the building would be empty of workers.

On the first night of my investigation, I climbed out of my patrol truck in the dark parking lot and met Lavon Benally, whom I jokingly called the Jailer on account of the massive ring of keys he carried. Lavon worked for the organization that had reported the haunting, and he had agreed to form part of my team for the weekend, primarily to show me around and to open the many doors of the building. Lavon was a sturdy

Navajo man in his sixties, very likeable and helpful. He was deeply religious but had experienced the paranormal events himself and was eager to get to the bottom of what was happening.

I had two other team members on their way. One was my cousin, Tony Milford Jr., the audiovisual wizard who had assisted with the San Juan River Bigfoot case. The other was Dusty Delgado, a non-Native paranormal investigator from Dallas whom Jon and I met by chance at a Lotaburger in New Mexico when he overheard us talking about Bigfoot. He had introduced himself to us and told us about his childhood experience seeing a Bigfoot and a UFO on the same day, as well as the Bigfoot activity he had witnessed while working on different ranches in Texas, New Mexico, and other states. I knew he would be helpful in a case like this, not only for his experience but also because he owned some high-tech equipment useful in these types of investigations. Between him and Tony, we would be bristling with electronics.

There would be four of us altogether, a sacred number in Navajo culture. Four represents the cardinal directions and the four sacred mountains that mark the borders of Navajoland: Blanca Peak, Mount Taylor, San Francisco Peaks, and Hesperus Mountain. I felt it was an auspicious way to proceed in this case, in which we were very likely to encounter ghosts, demons, or other spiritual energies.

But for now, it was just Lavon and I who went into the building to perform an initial walk-through and get the lay of the land. I wanted to get a feel for the environment and put a plan together before Dusty and Tony arrived at nine p.m. I was responsible for ensuring their safety, both physically and spiritually, so I needed to be prepared. I also needed a clear plan for how to conduct the investigation and how to collect any evidence we might encounter. Of course, despite my detailed planning and conference with the chief and Jon, investigating paranormal cases still required on-the-spot improvisation and adaptation—sometimes there was no standard operating procedure, and I had to make it up as I went along.

Lavon led me through the ground level of the building, where the organization had its offices, unlocking doors as he went. My sixth sense immediately stirred to life, recognizing something eerie and unnatural in the air—the spot above my right temple throbbed in that strange and unmistakable way. This was a sharp warning that a spiritual entity was near and that I needed to be on guard. Nothing had happened yet, but I already felt sure that something would, much in the same way you know that someone's about to pull a gun on you at a traffic stop.

We proceeded from the ground floor to the basement, which was a strange area, especially on the north end. The ceilings were about ten feet high, with exposed electrical conduits and water pipes. Mirrors covered the entirety of two walls. Apparently, the room had been intended as a gym at some point in the building's history. But now it contained only a large oval conference table.

Lavon went back upstairs to continue unlocking doors, and I paused in this room, leaning against the table, thinking over my plan of attack. Suddenly, I felt an invisible finger touch my upper lip. The finger moved slowly across my moustache, from one side to the other and then back again. I held completely still, though a jolt of excitement went through me. Goose bumps spread across my skin and the hair on the back of my neck stood up, an automatic physical reaction I couldn't control like I did my emotions. Something was clearly happening!

Before I could move or respond, I heard two distinct male voices, apparently in conversation, only about three feet to my left. There was no one there, but I could hear them and determined that they were Navajo based on their accents, tone, and inflection. I couldn't make out what they were saying, but it was a clear back-and-forth conversation that lasted approximately five to ten seconds.

I stood there for a long moment. "Who's there?" I asked.

No answer.

"Who are you?" I tried again.

No answer.

I tried a few more questions before giving up and going to find Lavon upstairs. I told him what had happened, and he smiled and said that was exactly the kind of experience he and the other workers had been having. I told him I would set up our center of operations in the basement conference room since it seemed to have clear paranormal activity. I was now certain that a spiritual entity was involved, though I wasn't entirely prepared to say it was ghosts. I didn't feel afraid, only excited. I felt once more like an explorer with the complete unknown ahead of me.

Later, when I had time to reflect, I would think back on my experiences as a young man in my mother's house—the lit stove burners, the sound of footsteps creeping through the house, furniture that was lifted and dropped. Finally, here was something to validate all of that and cast it into a larger context. But in that moment, I was too attuned to the activity happening in the building to think of anything else; all of my senses were engaged, just as they would be on a SWAT mission.

Tony and Dusty arrived soon after, bringing an astonishing amount of equipment with them—laptops and high-end video cameras of all varieties, infrared technology—you name it, they probably had it. It took thirty minutes just to unload all of it and set everything up in the conference room.

That done, I welcomed my team and briefed them on what I had already experienced before taking them on a walk-through of the building. A frisson of excitement spread within the group. Everyone here was deeply interested in exploring the paranormal and eager to see what we might discover. It was a different experience from working with fellow Rangers, most of whom wouldn't get within a hundred yards of a case like this on account of the deep Navajo taboos regarding the spirit world. That's partly why it was necessary to bring in outsiders to help with this case and others like it; the work I was doing was so unusual that we had to use unusual methods too, including who we recruited to help with our operations.

I had barely finished briefing the others when I felt a small, hard object hit my shoulder and plunk to the ground behind me.

I spun around, but no one was there. A quarter lay heads up on the floor. It had apparently fallen out of the sky. I looked up at the ceiling, as if to find someone hanging up there, bat-like, and grinning at me. But of course, it was just an empty ceiling.

Tony and I both took pictures of the quarter, and then I measured its dimensions and collected it—our first piece of evidence.

We moved southward through the basement floor into the next room. There was a newspaper rack of the sort you might see at the public library; it was blocking the aisle. I noticed it at the same time I heard another quarter fall, just behind it. I located the sound just in time to see the quarter spin and then fall on its side, once more with George Washington's profile face up. We again took photos and collected the evidence.

Yet I was skeptical. Why on earth would coins be raining out of thin air? That wasn't something I had experienced before. I took everyone back to the command room and asked that they empty their pockets and pull them out like rabbit ears to show me that they weren't carrying around a bunch of coins. It seemed far more likely that Dusty or Tony might be pranking me than that this was evidence of the paranormal. But no one was carrying change.

We were interested to see if the coins would appear in different rooms and under different circumstances, so we all filed into a women's bathroom on the main floor and turned out the lights. Perhaps the lack of light would prompt a response. As we waited in the darkness, the sound of coins hitting the floor began. One of us quickly turned the lights back on just in time to see more coins raining down. There were eight in total, of varying denominations: quarters, dimes, nickels, and pennies. They were all heads up.

Coins continued to apport, or appear from thin air, for the duration of our time investigating the government building. They fell whether the lights were on or off, and in many different rooms. In the bathrooms and basement areas, the floor was either tile or poured concrete, so we heard every coin as it made contact with the floor, each emitting a chime. In the cubicle area, where it was carpeted, the coins fell with soft, barely audible thuds. Sometimes the coins fell straight down, as if from the ceiling, and sometimes they came at us horizontally, as if thrown. In our command room in the basement, I witnessed a coin fly from the top southwest corner of the ten-foot ceiling all the way across the room to the floor, a distance of about thirty feet.

After the coins fell, they behaved normally. There was nothing special about their appearance. We could have taken them to the store and spent them like normal—but of course, we didn't do that! We photographed each coin and collected them as evidence. There were sixty-five coins that fell over the two-day period. Once, when we came back to our room in the basement, we discovered that the coins we had left on the desk had been stacked up into piles by an unseen hand.

It would be easy to think that someone had rigged up the coins to fall from the ceiling, and I certainly considered the possibility. But with at least ten of the coins, I saw the moment of their apporting, as they appeared from thin air right in front of my eyes. Because of those coins, I knew there was no way that someone was hoaxing us.

I couldn't imagine what the coins meant. Why were they falling? Was there anything special about them? And why were they all heads up?

The only conclusion I could draw was that a spirit was saying, "Heads up, I'm here."

Whoever or whatever it was, it certainly had our attention.

THE COINS WEREN'T the only physical manifestations we witnessed. It seemed like something new happened every ten minutes or so. We barely had time to ponder one encounter before another emerged. We never knew what might happen next.

Some of the most dramatic phenomena occurred in the large open area where the workers' cubicles were located. This room was once a theater, so there was a stage much like one you would see in a school auditorium, with a few wooden steps leading up to the platform. From there you could look over the entire room. Lining the stage was a glass railing with chrome accents. A large conference table filled the stage where performances were once held, task chairs arranged around it. Behind this was the director's office, which had a huge glass window with vertical blinds. It was a surprisingly beautiful space, especially decorated for the holidays as it was at this time, with green wreaths and colorful glass bulbs spread over the railing.

Yet it was absolutely haunted.

Standing on the main floor in front of the cubicles, facing the stage, the four of us watched as a task chair suddenly shot across the stage, rolling twelve to fifteen feet before hitting the railing with enough force to knock several of the Christmas bulbs to the floor.

There was no doubt: Something had moved the chair with force.

At the beginning of the investigation, we had systematically taken digital reference photos so that we could see if anything was later moved. I also took pictures from the stage with my Canon DSLR, with a wide lens, looking out over the cubicles. One of those photos showed something surprising: In the air over the cubicles hung hundreds of orbs, three-dimensional in appearance with different sizes and hues, like what you would see if a bubble-making machine were pumping soap bubbles into the air. At first, I assumed this was a mere artifact of the photo, an easily explained effect of light.

Then I used photo software to zoom in. All of the orbs had human faces.

I don't mean that they had something your brain could pattern into a face, as with pareidolia, or visual matrixing, which causes us to make meaningful patterns in everything we see, turning tree knots into eyes or the plug of a light switch into a smiling face.

I mean that they had *human* faces—real, distinct human faces, each one with individual features as different from one another as if they were living people in a room.

I didn't know what to make of it, but several consecutive photos showed the same. As an investigator, I try not to jump to conclusions. But I felt sure that each of those faces represented a human soul that had died. I didn't know how they came to be in this space or why, but I did feel that they were spirits—*hundreds* of spirits.

Who were they, and what did they want? I had no idea.

Whoever they were, the spirits seemed particularly fond of throwing things. On the second night, a very large and heavy battery from an early generation laptop came flying through the air and slammed into the partition wall of one of the cubicles, leaving a dent.

We also found evidence of a vase exploding. We had just come into the building on the second night, walking in as a group around nine p.m. We had barely walked through the foyer in the dark when we heard a loud crash and a sound like glass breaking. We were startled and stopped walking for a moment. But then Lavon hurried to turn on the lights in the reception area, and Dusty and Tony went through to the office cubicle area and flipped on those lights.

At the first cubicle on our left, we discovered that a ceramic vase had been smashed, and its pieces littered the top of the desk. As we studied the dispersal pattern of the pieces, we realized that the vase had actually exploded from within, as if someone had lit an M-80 firecracker inside it. But there was no evidence of human interference and no obvious explanation for how the vase came to be scattered in pieces on the desk.

Later on, when we studied our original photos taken on the first night, we found the vase—it was sitting four cubicles away on top of a file cabinet that belonged to the woman who had been getting the nonstop phone calls. It was a Navajo wedding vase with two spouts, the kind of gift that is usually given to a couple upon their marriage. Had the vase been moved by a spirit nearly forty feet across the room and then exploded from within? After what we'd seen, I had no trouble imagining it.

But what the meaning of the vase's destruction was, I didn't know. Was it a threat? An expression of frustration? Or simply a ploy for our attention?

We did our best to try to get the spirits to speak more clearly, performing a few different experiments designed to engage them. I rigged up a battery-operated microphone suspended within a loop on a long rod for Tony to carry. It fed into a recording device. If you listened in real time through headphones, you could turn up the volume to hear minute and ambient sounds. Tony wore this as he walked through the building, asking questions to see if anyone might respond. When he reached the kitchen area on the main floor, he finally received a response.

"Is anybody there?"

No response.

"Anyone there?" Tony tried again.

Just as he was about to walk out of the kitchen, someone answered.

"Yes, I'm here," a man's voice said. He spoke in English, but to me, when I listened to the recording on the digital voice recorder and later the digital copy, the voice sounded Navajo in tone and inflection. It sent goose bumps spreading over my skin.

"Can you tell me your name?" Tony asked.

The spirit gave his name, which I'm sorry to say that I can no longer recall. They talked for a few more moments before the spirit stopped responding. Unfortunately, he wasn't able to tell us why he was there or what he might want.

However, listening back to the audio, we could tell that the spirit was giving active, intelligent, and deliberate responses to Tony's questions. It wasn't like a tape being played back, as in some residual hauntings. This was a conscious being *choosing* to interact with Tony.

As I listened to the recording again and again, my mind was swimming, trying to make sense of it. How could a spirit process a communicated question? One would surmise that this would require a thought process. Living humans have a brain to perform this function. But how could a spirit do the same? Yes, the spirit was once a living person, but now as a ghost it does not have a body, with a head and a cranium that houses a brain, or a mouth or vocal cords to create speech and words. So how was it possible? I didn't know, but it was certainly happening.

Tony also left an electronic voice recorder on the table of the large conference room in the basement, hoping to get an Electronic Voice Phenomena (EVP) recording. He set it to record and then went upstairs. When he returned and played it back, there was a loud noise like a large piece of furniture being moved around on the cement floor. Then, a female voice with a crisp British-sounding accent said, "Guess what?"

Later on, when I played this recording while at a conference in Scotland, a local recognized the accent as a particular Scottish dialect.

Why was there a Scottish woman's voice in a government building in the Navajo Nation? I can only offer conjecture. Maybe she was a nurse or someone who worked in the morgue during one of the pandemics. Non-Native medical people have been present on the reservation since the cavalry set up here in the 1800s. Perhaps she was one of them. I've heard other stories about Anglo women dressed as nurses whose ghosts haunt places on the reservation. A medicine man told me about one who haunted a particular highway, where she had crashed and died many years before. I know there have been several incidents of assault and murder of nurses that have occurred here on the Navajo Reservation. I don't know the details, such as nationality or how long ago these incidents happened, but perhaps something like this is to blame for the presence of nurses' spirits on the reservation.

We also had a rather strange finding with the electromagnetic field (EMF) meter, which, as explained in the previous chapter, is a tool that is often used in paranormal investigations to detect the presence of spirits and other supernatural phenomena. Tony and I were walking through the basement in the pitch dark with only the backlit orange light of the EMF meter to guide us. Pain flared above my temple, bringing me to intense alertness. *Something* was here. We were in the same room where we had seen the coin fall near the newspaper rack. It was a file room filled with shelves of labeled binders. The number on the EMF meter was constantly moving—cycling through hundreds or even thousands of frequencies—until it suddenly stopped at the number 666 and held there for a full ten seconds.

Our faces lit a lurid orange, Tony and I looked at each other. I saw the same jolt of shock and unease in his eyes that I felt in my chest. I had used that scanner many times before, but it had never locked on a single frequency for that length of time and never *that* number.

The numbers started cycling again, but then a few steps later, the EMF meter stopped again.

666.

We held the reader up to the exposed wires overhead to make sure it wasn't a naturally occurring frequency.

It wasn't. The numbers cycled as usual.

The 666 reading didn't seem to be reflecting anything in the environment. Rather, it felt like someone was trying to frighten us with the number of the Beast from the Book of Revelation, a number associated with Satan and the Antichrist and all that is evil. Having been raised in the Baptist tradition on my mom's side of the family, I well understood the meaning of the message. An ominous feeling overtook us as we realized the ill-intent of the spirit or energies around us.

The threat certainly worked on Tony, who was thoroughly freaked out, but after my initial shock faded, I laughed it off. If it was meant to be a message of intimidation or threat, it wasn't a particularly strong one. Even Lavon, who was very religious, was completely unfazed by it. A number couldn't hurt us. It was much less impressive than that exploding vase.

The 666 wasn't the only time a number came into play. A lot of the paranormal activity happened at around three a.m., and in one instance, the clock in the file room in the basement also stopped at exactly three a.m. just as something supernatural occurred. I do know this clock was working as I had observed it several times during the course of the investigation prior to it stopping. Three in the morning is, of course, the witching hour. The clock never restarted.

What was it the spirit or energies present here wanted, I continued to wonder. At times the activity seemed angry and aggressive, but the behavior was more like a petulant child acting out than anything truly malevolent. There were no simple or easy answers; only puzzling demands for our attention, which went on incessantly throughout the night.

Most of the activity happened on its own, independent of us, but some of it we did attempt to provoke. One such experiment involved an eight-inch fluorescent lime green rubber ball, the type you see in a dollar store, intended for bouncing. We placed it in the middle of a hallway in a location where one of the government employees had heard a disembodied voice. We left cameras to monitor the ball to see if anything would happen to it. The camera captured the ball moving on its own down the hall and out of frame. We later found the ball thirty feet away stuffed inside a forty-gallon trash can. The trash can was located right next to the clock that had stopped working at three a.m.

Hallways were a frequent site of eerie happenings. Once, the four of us were going down the stairs to the base station in the basement, snapping pictures as we went. Dusty was at the back of the line when a four-foot sign slapped him on the back. It was one of those black lined signs that you can stick little white letters on, and due to its metal base, it was heavy. Dusty yelped when it hit him. The spirits seemed to have a particular interest in Dusty. Another time in the hallway, our cameras clearly captured a disembodied hand floating behind Dusty's head, its pale fingers reaching for him.

Even before I heard the Navajo man's voice responding to Tony's questions, I had known that we were dealing with a dynamic and active haunting. In fact, I had suspected from the beginning that the haunting involved an intelligent, aware spiritual entity of some kind, one who was conscious of what was happening and able to manipulate its environment and interact with the living humans around it.

At one point prior to the two nights of investigation, I was speaking with Lavon, who was in Monument Valley. While we were talking, I had another call coming in and saw that it was the woman who had been receiving the strange phone calls at her desk. After I hung up with Lavon, I called her back, asking what she needed. She said she hadn't called me. When I insisted I'd received a call from her desk phone, she told me that she was in the director's office at the time of the call and could see into her cubicle from there. No one was at her desk. No one had used her phone.

Whatever entity was in the building was already reaching out to me, even before the investigation had begun. I only hoped that once we left the building, it wouldn't follow me home. But my law enforcement training had taught me to hope for the best and prepare for the worst.

After the two nights of investigation, I debriefed with the director, telling her everything we had seen and discovered. At that point, she opened up for the first time, sharing the experiences she had had while at work. My findings had validated her own experiences enough for her to feel comfortable sharing them. Apart from disclosing our discoveries, there wasn't much more I could do for her or her employees. I gave her the contact information for a medicine man and wished her well. I hoped that would be the end of it—but, of course, it wasn't.

The night following the investigation, around nine p.m., Dusty and I were sitting at the dining room table in my home, processing some of the images we had taken, when an object fell behind my chair in the kitchen, pinging against the linoleum. Shocked by the familiar sound, I spun around and searched the floor for a coin, which I soon found. It was a quarter, and it lay heads up. Dusty looked over at me, his eyes huge. I grabbed my camera and took a picture of the quarter.

Excited, Dusty jumped up from the table and grabbed his own camera. He began taking photographs of my entire residence to have a record of its state for later comparison. Just as he came out of my bedroom, as he crossed the threshold, I looked up from my own camera to see five coins fall over his head. One of them was very hot to the touch when I picked it up. Looking down at the floor, I realized that the coin had left an impression in the linoleum, leaving a ring of black outlined on the floor.

Oh shit! I thought to myself.

The haunting had indeed followed me back to my home, where it would remain. The coins continued to fall, each of them heads up. And my home became a place of strange paranormal activity, which is still going on today. Objects were moved and knocked over. I could sometimes hear things running across the roof, too heavy to be squirrels. My previously quiet and peaceful home had been invaded.

The next day after the coins first fell, I called my cousin Tony. I said, "You'll never guess what's happening at my house."

Tony laughed. "Is it coins?"

It turned out that it was happening at his house in Fort Defiance too. In fact, he experienced some of the worst of the ongoing haunting. He had coins flying across the room, as well as household objects. A pair of large toenail clippers flew from the bathroom to the hallway and slammed into the wall hard enough to tear the wallpaper.

Once, while I was at his house, I witnessed something even more alarming. We were walking into the kitchen, me in front and Tony a few feet behind, when a twelve-inch butcher's knife flew from the knife block on the kitchen counter and traveled six feet across the room, stabbing into a grapefruit in a hanging wire basket about three feet from me. The knife had stabbed hard enough to pierce all the way through the grapefruit.

Tony started to swear, his eyes wide.

He was understandably shaken up by these events, but I told him that the spirit was clearly only trying to send a message. If it had wanted to hurt us, it certainly could have. Instead, it was only after our attention.

But the spirit activity continued unabated. One day Tony's elderly mother and older brother Brandon came by his house while I was there. We were all sitting on a large sectional couch. Brandon was expressing his skepticism about our paranormal experiences at the government building.

"Well, hell, if it's going to throw money, at least it could throw some damn bills," he joked.

No sooner had he said this than a wadded-up dollar bill hit his mother on the cheek. When we smoothed the paper out, we saw the word DIE had been written in Sharpie marker in all capital letters, with the horizontal lines of the E extending out like pitchfork prongs.

At this point, Tony became terrified for his young daughter's safety. She lived with her mother but stayed with him on the weekends. He felt he needed to get the haunting out of his home immediately. A friend of his, who was quite religious, told him about a pastor from Oklahoma who was holding a revival in Fort Defiance and who was known to be accomplished in exorcisms. She suggested having the pastor over, and Tony was desperate enough to agree.

The pastor came, bringing xeroxed prayers with him, which were passed out to everyone. We all prayed together, reciting from the papers. Then we went outside and built a fire, where we would burn the coins and the dollar bill that had appeared in Tony's home. Tony sprinkled the coins into the fire. I pulled the bill from my pocket and dropped it into the fire. When the bill hit the fire, it blew up like a firecracker, scattering embers into the air. I laughed, impressed by the strength of the haunting.

There was no more spirit activity at Tony's after that. The heavy, oppressive feeling that had filled the house was now gone.

My house was a different story. Years later, I am still experiencing the ongoing effects of the haunting. Coins appear throughout my home and sometimes even fall near me when I'm out in public—in broad daylight. They have fallen at the laundromat, in convenience stores, and in restaurants. One morning, a gentleman standing next to me in a Love's Travel Stop witnessed a coin fall on the floor within two feet of him and me. I knew he clearly saw the coin apport out of thin air based on the shocked look on his face. His eyes were as wide as saucers and his mouth was hanging open as he stood frozen. I smiled sheepishly at him and leaned over and picked up the coin. I stepped over to the cashier, paid for my orange juice and muffin, and left. I said nothing, but after I got into my truck, I couldn't help but laugh at his expression.

I had assumed the spirits were taking coins from the physical places they manifested and dropping them near me, except that once a Taiwanese coin appeared in my home, and I could not think of any way to account for its presence since I didn't have any coins like that. Later on, as I will share in the next chapter, the coins fell in a remote, isolated location, far from any cash register or pockets. This completely disrupted my theory of the coins' origins.

I try to keep the energies under control by cedaring my home regularly, a form of cleansing and blessing more commonly known as smudging. I take a tiny, three-inch cast-iron skillet, put charcoal into it and light it, then sprinkle either dried or fresh cedar over it. It smokes intensely, especially when I use fresh cedar, and I use an eagle feather to fan the smoke. Smudging is a common practice, ritual, or type of simple ceremony of Native Americans, First Nations people, and other Indigenous peoples. The act of burning cedar, sweetgrass, Palo Santo, or even incense releases smoke containing negative ions, which can have the effect of removing toxic or harmful energies from our body, mind, and spirit and from our immediate environment, such as our car or home. This is an act of cleansing, blessing, or protection. The key is that there must be an accompanying intent or intention along with the act of smudging. Simply going through the act of smudging will not have the desired effect without meaningful intent.

At conferences, Jon Dover and I are often asked by non-Natives if they should use this ritual themselves. However, we recommend that non-Natives research and learn what their ancestors practiced in their own culture to conduct a cleansing or blessing, or spiritual protection, rather than just copying another culture whose rituals may not work for a person outside of the community or culture. Additionally, eagle feathers are protected by US law, which prohibits their possession, use, and sale. Many Native people can legally possess eagle feathers, which are commonly used for smudging rituals, though sometimes a fan made of other types of feathers is used to direct and control the smoke.

I am grateful to the Creator and my tribe for providing me with a personal practice that offers me protection and puts my mind at ease when dealing with supernatural cases. That said, the ongoing Window Rock haunting doesn't really bother me; I don't believe there is anything to truly be feared. In most haunting cases, the spirit is that of a former living person and generally does not possess the intent or ability to inflict serious harm on people. There are other entities or energies out there that were never human at any point, and these can be quite dangerous and should be left to a professional to deal with. However, I have never felt I was dealing with something of that nature in my home. In some cases, a spirit will try to evoke fear and will feed off our fear, as with the spirit that caused my EMF meter to show the number 666 to frighten Tony and me. But I am able to control my responses and not give in to fear in these instances.

In fact, I later ended up working in that very office building in Window Rock—in the basement room where something had run a finger over my moustache. The Rangers were moved to the building after I started getting intense migraines while at work and the EPA discovered black mold in the wall of my office. I much preferred ghosts to toxic mold poisoning, so I wasn't too bothered. I laughed and said, "Oh, here we go!"

I did continue to experience haunting phenomena in the building during the years I worked there. Once, when I was cleaning the fridge after someone had left meat in it for too long, I looked down at my arm and watched a deep scratch form quickly on my skin as if an invisible cat's talon were running straight down it, a thin line of blood following the invisible claw. It stung just like a cat's scratch would too. After I finished with the refrigerator, I cleaned the wound carefully. The mark lasted for a few weeks, but it did not leave a permanent scar. That was probably the most disturbing of the events in my office, though there were many.

I was usually the first to arrive in the morning and was frequently there at nighttime as a result of SWAT operations. Once, before Halloween, I was there very late, sitting at a conference table in the chief's office, working on some paperwork. I happened to look up and saw someone reflected in the swinging glass doors—standing right behind me. It was a person dressed as a Civil War soldier. I quickly covered my sidearm and turned, but there was no one there. Someone who lived near the building later told me they'd also seen a Civil War soldier outside the building.

Another time, I found upside-down children's handprints on the blackboard in my office. The handprints were in the stairwell too, at about waist height on a dusty shelf. When I mentioned it to others, I started hearing stories that might explain the handprints. Lavon told me that when he had worked in the building, he saw a little girl dressed in late-1800s clothing of the type worn at a Bureau of Indian Affairs boarding school. He said his son, who was a child at the time, saw the little girl too one night when they were in the building late.

The custodian in our building also had a story about a little girl ghost. He said he witnessed a girl in a white dress who was pushing his cleaning cart across the room. Other government buildings in the area reported similar occurrences. People who worked at the fire department and the education center saw the exact same little girl.

Once, when Robert Allan, the attorney for the Navajo Nation Division of Natural Resources, and I were sitting in his office, which is also in Window Rock, we heard a sound like a rubber ball bouncing right in front of us. From the sound, it was clear that it was being bounced right in front of us, in our immediate presence. But we did not see anything or anyone there. Robert said that his boss had witnessed two children's ghosts playing with a ball in the hallway.

I know that many people find the ghosts of children especially frightening, perhaps because of how they have been depicted in popular horror movies. However, the spirits of children make me feel only empathy and a desire to comfort them. Just as most children want the presence of their biological parent, especially their mother, I believe that when the spirit of a child is present it could be trying to find its way to its parents or mother. I think child spirits should be treated with the same gentleness, kindness, and softspoken manner with which we treat living children. Some spirits of children may not be aware or conscious of the fact that they have passed on. They may just have the sense that they are somehow lost and alone. I believe that is probably what the child ghosts in Window Rock are experiencing.

The sightings of these child spirits and the other ghostly events took place over a period of about eight years. I asked my friend, who is a medicine man, why he thought the hauntings were occurring in this area. He said this area near Window Rock has attracted human activity for a long, long time. Many, many different peoples have lived their lives here, from the Anasazi to present day. Additionally, the Navajos, who were removed from their homes during the Long Walk, were encamped in and around Window Rock before being marched to Fort Sumner. People were shot, bayoneted, raped, and killed in this place. There was a great deal of turmoil, going far back in our history. That energy doesn't just disappear like smoke. The turmoil and pain of those people were retained by the environment, turning it into a paranormal hotspot. Centuries later, their energy can still be felt.

The Long Walk's legacy permeates the Navajo Nation. When I drive to Albuquerque and I'm looking at the beautiful landscape, I can't help but imagine the Navajos who marched this way on their return from the Long Walk, how they looked at the sacred peak of Mount Taylor just as I am looking at it now and knew that they were returning home. After months of hardship, hunger, and pain, displaced from their rightful lands, they now saw the red rocks and the incredible sunset and felt the sense of home in their bones.

In the same way, I cannot help but feel compassion for the spirits who are bound to this land. They were once living people just like me, and one day I will leave this plane of existence too. Now, in my late fifties, their presence only reminds me of how fleeting life is and forces me to be grateful for this life I get to live now. At times I feel like there are spirits who know me nearby, watching over me and guiding me. Perhaps they are warning me to be aware and cautious. I've even wondered if it might be my mother's spirit staying close to me.

Their presence connects me to what has gone before and reminds me not to forget those we have lost. Perhaps that is all that the spirits who linger in haunted places want; perhaps that is what they are saying when they drop coins and throw objects and reach through other worlds to touch us. Perhaps they are saying, "I am here. Do not forget me."

CHAPTER 10

Theories of a Navajo Ranger

OVER THE YEARS, WITH EACH CASE I INVESTIGATED, I HAD *AHA!* moments and epiphanies, each one moving my thinking about the paranormal forward a little bit more. But the falling coins in the Window Rock haunting case were the key to opening my mind to the underlying commonality of all of the paranormal events I had investigated over the course of my career. The coins came from *somewhere*, manifesting into our physical world. It made me realize that there must be other dimensions occupying the same space that we are. The coins seemed to appear out of nothingness, but they must have some origin, some way of being moved from one place to another.

Then, a few years later, an event occurred in which the coins appeared in a totally unrelated context during a completely different paranormal investigation, taking my thoughts about dimensions and other worlds to a whole new level.

It was March 2014 and I had been called out to the home of a woman named Geneva who lived near Twin Buttes close to Navajo, New Mexico, about twelve miles north of Fort Defiance. Her home was in the Chuska Mountains, an area with an elevation of about 8,000 feet. Geneva had reported Bigfoot activity around her residence to my cousin Tony, who asked me and Dusty to come out with him to investigate. She said that her family had witnessed Bigfoot activity year-round for a long time. Two or three of the woman's family members also described seeing strange creatures around their home and having sticks thrown at them. I thought there was a decent chance it actually was a Bigfoot, though I also had to consider the possibility of witchcraft and skinwalkers.

We drove out to the family's home to take their statements and conducted an investigation there, but we didn't find anything of interest around their property. They suggested that we drive up to the mountains, where they had recently witnessed Bigfoot activity and felt sure that we would find the creature. A few of the family members accompanied us to act as guides, directing me as I drove about four miles from their home and up, up, up into the mountains. It was already dark by the time we arrived at our destination, and the temperature had dropped quickly, leaving the air cold and clear. The mountains were filled with enormous, towering ponderosa pines, many of them three- to four-feet thick at their bases. It was a very high elevation with primitive logging roads, and we were glad to have a four-wheel-drive truck for the journey.

The smell of the forest was powerful, sharp and clear, as it often is in high, green places where humans rarely go. There was an eerie silence hanging in the cold air. There were no sounds of animals or birds, hardly even wind in the trees. It felt like being in a void or vacuum. For those unused to this environment, it can be quite unnerving, as the sensation is like having earplugs in one's ears. In some cases, this can affect a person's equilibrium, giving them the sense of being almost intoxicated—or make them sick. But everyone on this mission was used to the terrain.

Once we were quite high up the mountain, we reached a junction and took the southward road, which had a gradual slope. Before we got out of the truck, I held a quick briefing so that everyone would be aware of a contingency plan should any unforeseen incidents arise, such as an injury or a hazardous situation. From here on out, we would remain as quiet as possible, with no unnecessary moving or even talking, unless there was a real need to communicate. We took night vision goggles and external flashlights with infrared lenses, which were very powerful and able to see long-distance.

The one exception to our rule of silence was that Tony and Dusty performed a few experiments with audio and visual equipment, hoping to provoke a response. This included playing prerecorded Bigfoot calls. They also used wood-knocking, in which a thick branch or pipe is struck on a semi-hollow log or tree to produce a loud knocking sound. Tony and Dusty often used these types of activities in their own investigations, but Jon and I typically didn't like to provoke the creatures or entities we sought or try to elicit a response with negative stimuli. I suppose this difference of approach lies in our primary reasons for investigating the paranormal: Tony and Dusty investigated because they were interested, whereas Jon and I investigated because it was our jobs.

I didn't interfere with Tony and Dusty's experiments, but I chose to act as observer and recorder rather than participant. I did witness repeated clear responses to both activities, primarily the sound of something incredibly heavy walking and moving nearby, breaking large branches under its feet. *Holy shit*, I thought—after listening for a while, I was sure that the noises were Bigfoot and not just the wind or wildlife. A chemical cocktail of adrenaline and excitement was flowing through my veins.

Sometime after midnight, we started hearing animal sounds like those made by a bear or wolf—a low, deep growling that made the hairs on our necks stand on end. With the NVGs, I scanned the tree line, searching for the source of the noise. There was movement in the trees and brush. I spotted something between fifty and a hundred yards away. It was standing upright, watching us from behind a stand of ponderosa pines. My heart rate spiked, all my attention now laser-focused on the figure lurking in the green-hued darkness.

It seemed to be studying us intently too. As we waited, it started moving toward us, still mostly hidden behind the trees—flashes of movement, a large dark outline against the shadowy darkness. Its eyes reflected the light of the infrared flashlight, an intense and intelligent stare. As it emerged from a gap in the branches, I saw it clearly. The creature had features like that of a bear and a gorilla, as well as a human. It was well over six feet tall and covered all over in dark hair. Its arms were very long and made human-like movements. It had hardly any neck, seeming to be all head, a bit like a gorilla. It was walking upright with a human-like gait, not at all like a bear on its hind legs. I could see some of its facial features, which certainly did not belong to any man or animal I'd ever seen.

My mind immediately flashed back to the story that Teddy Roosevelt told about the Bigfoot that sank its fangs into a man and broke his neck with its bare hands. For a moment, my racing heart was all I could hear, blood pounding in my ears, breath held.

As an investigator, skepticism is built in, so I had to watch the creature for a long time, letting my mind take it all in before I was sure that what I was seeing was real. There was a very strong sense of shock and disbelief, my mind and my body warring for dominance. My skeptical mind was telling me that it couldn't be real, but my eyes were telling me, "Yes, it *is* real, and it's right there in front of you."

With that realization, so many thoughts and emotions flooded me at once. My gut instinct or sixth sense was trying to decide what I needed to do to keep myself and everyone else safe. Then my SWAT training was telling me to remain calm and use tactical breathing methods as I had been trained—breathe in and count to ten; hold my breath and count to ten; exhale and count to ten; repeat, repeat, repeat until I was calm. But I knew I was seeing something that didn't fit within the normal context of life. It wasn't a bear or a man. It was something otherworldly, a creature straight out of the tales I'd heard since childhood. It was Bigfoot—*Yé'iitsoh*—real and in the flesh, right before my eyes.

This was the creature I had hunted and tracked, whose footprints I had taken castings of and whose hair I'd had analyzed in a lab. I'd been following its breadcrumbs all these years. But now, I was face-to-face with it, seeing it just as it had likely seen me all this time, lurking unseen in the periphery of human civilization. Finally, here was irrefutable proof: *Bigfoot was real.*

My senses were electrified as I stared at it and it stared at me, both of us waiting to see what would happen next. The creature didn't seem in any danger of charging us, so I passed the NVGs to the others to have a look. I kept my carbine rifle close, but I didn't think I would need to use it. My body's instinctive reaction of fear and wariness had morphed into pure exhilaration.

I watched it with a FLIR, or Forward-Looking Infrared, thermal scope, which is a camera-like device that sees heat signatures in great detail. For example, if you used it to look at the wall of a house, you could see the two-by-fours and studs in the wall because they have a different heat signature than the drywall. With the FLIR I could clearly see details of the creature's hair, the different texture it had against the surrounding forest. The creature was so *real* and so present—its existence now undeniable.

It slowly began to advance toward us again, climbing up the hill. We could hear it moving through the forest, crunching limbs and brush—not just twigs but large branches. It sounded very, very heavy. I readied myself for . . . well I didn't know for what. A confrontation? An attack? But then it stopped moving, and I lost sight of it.

In the space between one breath and the next, the Bigfoot was gone. We couldn't locate it again. It was as if the creature had vanished into thin air the same way the coins had appeared from nothingness in the Window Rock haunting case.

I felt sure that the Bigfoot had passed not merely out of our sight and hearing but out of our world. It had stepped out of our dimension and into another one, as inaccessible to us as the stars.

We continued in the woods for another hour, but we couldn't catch sight of the creature again. It was gone. Around two or three in the morning, we gave up and went home. But that was not the end of our contact with this particular Bigfoot, nor was it the final sighting of the species I would have.

Dusty and I returned the following day, driving up the rugged, steep terrain in his pickup truck. It was a bright, clear day, the sky an endless blue. We parked the truck and climbed out, still electrified by the events of the previous night. We walked down the incline to where we had seen the Bigfoot lurking among the ponderosa pines the night before.

We could find no sign of the creature. There was too much wild-life activity to determine whether any disturbances on the forest floor originated from the Bigfoot, and there were no footprints in the fallen leaves and needles. Undeterred, we went back toward Dusty's truck, scanning the ground for foot track evidence. We decided to walk down the dirt road, to the base of the mountain. We carried a digital recorder and watched the ground carefully. But there was simply no evidence to collect, so we started the walk back up.

When we were part of the way back up the slope, a sandstone rock suddenly flew toward us, as if thrown from down at ground level, a good five hundred feet below us. It was about a fourth the size of a baseball and landed with a small thud within ten feet of us. After a moment, another rock followed it, again landing ten feet away.

I smiled and looked at Dusty. I *knew* we were getting activity now.

Dusty's eyes went wide. "What the hell?" he said. "Where're those coming from?"

We tried to find the source of the rocks, using binoculars to peer down below. The rocks were clearly originating from far down the slope, possibly from the base of the mountain. But there was no one we could see, and the rocks kept coming. Whoever—or whatever—was throwing them didn't seem to be trying to hit us, but the rocks were clearly thrown with accuracy and intent, as if to warn us away.

As we went up the hill, the rocks continued, growing larger and larger in size. The possibility that a human being could be throwing them became increasingly impossible. Dusty was freaking out, but I stayed calm, simply collecting as many of the rocks as I could. When we reached the level where Dusty's truck was parked, the final and biggest rock of all came hurtling through the trees, the sound of it like a shot cannonball. We could hear it before we saw it—snapping all the branches in its path. It hit the soft earth about ten feet in front of us with an enormous thud. The thing was about thirty pounds, six inches thick, and twelve by fourteen inches in size. It was solid sandstone.

I calmly took pictures of the rock and kept searching for the place it had originated for another half hour or so. I couldn't figure out how a human could possibly get a rock of this size launched up the mountain at such a distance, even with a trebuchet. That's why I knew it wasn't human—it was a Bigfoot, likely urging us to go away and leave him in peace. He could have killed us with those rocks if he'd wanted to, and a threat was clearly implied: *I could crush you like bugs if I wanted to.*

Dusty was ready to get the hell out of there. He put down the gate of his truck to load our equipment, when suddenly, like a shotgun blast, came the sound of coins raining down in the bed of the truck and on top of the mounted toolbox. They'd come from the north, behind us and over our heads, from the same direction the rocks had been thrown. There were ten of them, all heads up.

I stood frozen for a long moment, truly shocked for the first time on this day of strange events. I had not expected coins to start apporting way out here in the mountains—especially not raining down on us like a hailstorm. It was incredible to witness the coins falling and glinting in the bright noontime sunshine, so utterly out of place. But I was also completely thrown. I didn't know what to think. I didn't have a ready answer to explain this, either to Dusty or to myself. But on the heels of the previous night's Bigfoot sighting and the morning's interaction with the creature, I felt the importance of this manifestation—it meant *something*, but I couldn't yet grasp what.

We got in the truck to leave before the Bigfoot made good on his threats or anything else happened. No sooner had the engine revved to life than another handful of coins rained down over the truck cab and windshield, pinging above our heads. I dutifully climbed back out to collect them.

Dusty yelled and cussed, more freaked out than ever, but I only laughed. It was hard not to be delighted by all of this—two paranormal cases converging in the strangest possible way. What did the coins have to do with the Bigfoot, if anything?

I thought about this as we drove back down the mountain, trying to work out what the connection might be. Was a spirit trying to warn us that we were in danger? Was some larger force at play? There must be some connection. It couldn't merely be a coincidence that two paranormal events would happen at the same time and place.

I couldn't work out what the connection might be, but the event drove home for me more than ever that there truly were other dimensions, perhaps even stacked on ours times infinity—worlds on worlds on worlds. And there were beings who could reach through those dimensions, whether spirits or Bigfoot or UFOs.

Bigfoot seems like such an earthly creature—large, mammalian, apelike, covered in hair. But there is no evidence of the creatures living longterm in the woods, like a mere cryptid in hiding. I can easily go out and track a bear or a cougar and find evidence of their habitations, but I cannot find evidence that Bigfoot lives in the places it has been sighted. As common and frequent as the sightings are worldwide, it should also be very common to see bones and remains of these beings. Yet no evidence like this has ever been found. But now I had watched it appear and disappear with my own eyes. So, I had to conclude that, like the coins appearing from someplace unseen, it too had stepped out of another dimension and into our world. And then it stepped back out.

After all, the Navajo creation stories include different worlds, different layers of existence, planes of being besides our own. In our creation narrative, the *Dine' Bahane'*, or Story of the People, Navajos are said to have emerged into our world through a giant reed after traveling through three other worlds—what is that if not dimensional travel?

What if nearly all the paranormal phenomena I'd investigated over the years were merely entities from other dimensions stepping briefly into ours? The orbs of light that are commonly seen on the Navajo Reservation could be coming from an entirely different universe; they could even be sent by UFOs. Maybe Bigfoot was sent by UFOs too since many people report seeing them in conjunction. Perhaps orbs and Bigfoot played a similar role, like drones collecting information to carry back to other beings.

Hell, I'd even heard stories on the reservation about people seeing dinosaurs. What if things from our own historical past could pass through a tear in time and space and wander into our present world?

What if that was the explanation for the Loch Ness Monster? Did this mean that teleportation was physically possible, from a physics standpoint? Were time and space more permeable than I had imagined?

Technically, I realized, a Ouija board could constitute a gateway to other dimensions. One can open a doorway or window to other dimensions and hopefully close the same opening after the session is completed. Of course, users have little control over who or what is going to come through that opening. It could be the spirit of a deceased person or loved one or a nonhuman evil or demonic entity. Imagine using a Ouija board in a paranormal hotspot—there is no telling who or what a person might make contact with.

The more I thought and the more my mind took in all the possibilities of existence, a great awe overtook me, an overwhelming sense of the vast infinity of the universe. I realized that human beings were like an ant colony in an isolated place. The ants never had contact with humans and thought their colony was the whole of existence. But, of course, there was a whole, huge, pulsing world outside the colony, unknown to them. Likewise, our universe contains a span of space so vast human beings might never encounter other life-forms unless they seek us out.

And by being so caught up in human concerns, in the materialistic realities of modern life with its workaday schedule and digital distractions and petty concerns, what were we ignoring? What were we forgetting?

I began to think about how humankind prides itself on moving away from so-called primitive belief systems, magical thinking, and superstition and toward logic and science. But what wisdom and knowledge were we losing? Just on the Navajo Reservation, we have fewer medicine men than we used to and even fewer medicine men who have been reared from childhood for the role, as they were in the past, steeped in shamanic culture, ritual, and history. Thus, the knowledge to undo certain curses has been lost; the songs and chants and medicine that would break that curse and provide healing for its victim have been forgotten. Perhaps this is why medicine men cannot break the curses in paranormal hotspots such as the government building in Window Rock. We have allowed Western society to eat away at Navajo culture, to take away our traditions and history and old ways of knowing. And that has left us vulnerable.

How much knowledge has been lost? How much skill? We inherited a paranormal world from our ancestors, but we do not have their knowledge or tools to help us deal with it. Those who painted the pictographs on the red rocks of Navajoland knew things we do not know. We think of ourselves as so advanced, but there are situations our ancestors could have handled that we cannot because we have allowed their knowledge to be lost. And we have allowed our lives and societies to become radically unbalanced. Before the colonization of North America, tribes lived in harmony with the land and one another; everyone had a valuable role in society and lived in proper balance, or *hózhó*. We have fallen so far from this ideal.

Having been raised between the Western and Navajo cultures, I recognized this loss keenly. I also felt a sense of duty and responsibility begin to settle over me. As a Navajo Ranger, I was an ambassador for the Navajo Nation. Likewise, as a paranormal investigator, I was an ambassador of the paranormal. As a law enforcement officer, I took an oath to be honest and ethical and to help people. I realized that I must share this knowledge with people. I must let others know about the paranormal events happening all around us. And I must urge a return to the Indigenous teaching of harmony and balance.

All things in the universe are interconnected. There are universal opposite elements of positive and negative energy, or forces, that are found throughout the universe, including within other dimensions. These are opposing forces that cannot exist without the other. Like a battery, these polar opposites can be found in almost all aspects of life.

You have night and day, yin and yang, black and white, cold and hot, light and dark, good and evil, and so many others. From this overall principle I feel that *all* things that are referred to as evil originate from one single source, but take many, many different forms throughout our world and the universe; and I feel the same for positive energy. The goal is to keep these forces in balance both in our own lives and in the world at large.

Clearly, something in our human culture has gone wrong. These paranormal events—UFO visitations, Bigfoot sightings, and hauntings— are happening at unprecedented rates for a reason. I have come to see them as a wake-up call for humankind—an *awakening*. Our planet is in crisis, multiple countries are at war, we have mass drug-overdose epidemics, and so many people are suffering. We must recognize how out of balance our world and lives are, how grotesque our treatment of the earth and one another is. And we must live better. We must do better. We must come back into balance with our environment and find clarity of purpose.

I want people who experience paranormal events to take them seriously and to examine why the event might be happening. I want them, first of all, to know that they are not crazy and that what they are experiencing may very well be real. But I also don't want them to be afraid. Feeding a paranormal entity our fear is to give it our energy. I want them to treat the event with caution and respect, knowing that all things have a soul. And I want them to consider whether their lives are in harmony and balance and to look for places where changes may be needed.

I am sometimes asked where the line is—how far my belief in the paranormal extends. This question is wrongheaded because for me, as I hope I have demonstrated throughout this book, the paranormal is not a matter of belief but of reality. I have seen these things with my own eyes and investigated them with all the tools at my disposal as a law enforcement officer and a Navajo. I do not *believe* in the paranormal; rather, I acknowledge its reality. My skepticism is as intact as it ever was, but I no longer doubt the existence of powers beyond our comprehension.

That said, I will answer the question: There is no line.

I'll say it again: *There is no line.*

Mythology is rooted in the real. Cultures all over the world have similar paranormal beings, even if those cultures have never had contact with one another. How can I acknowledge skinwalkers in Navajo culture but not vampires in European cultures, which have rituals to ward off vampires just as Navajos ward off the evil energies of witchcraft? How can I accept the Little People from Hopi culture but not fairies in England and Ireland?

In prizing Western culture and values, we have abandoned old ways of knowing. Of course, there are many contributions from Western culture that have made our world much better, such as lifesaving medicines and the scientific method. But we have forgotten so much. And that loss of knowledge and perspective makes us vulnerable, shortsighted, and small-minded.

In Indigenous belief, all things are connected; *nothing* stands alone and separate. So, I must look for the connections in the paranormal. When I witness a doppelgänger or see orbs in the night sky or hear a coin plunk onto the ground behind me, I stop and pay attention. I ask, *Why?* I ask, *What have I been missing?* I ask, *How can I live my life better and how can I be a better person?*

I do not have all the answers—far from it. I still cannot tell you why I experienced Bigfoot and falling coins at the same moment. I have endless theories, some that I'm fairly certain are accurate and others that are only hypotheses. Each case opened up my eyes a little bit more and a little bit more. Each case brought me closer to the knowledge of the world that has been stolen from Indigenous people by colonizers and lost to the passage of time and the evolution of Native cultures.

Here are some of the primary theories I have come to accept over the years, the ones I can put forth with confidence based on my own investigations and personal experiences, as well as traditional Navajo teachings:

1. Our world is not the only one. The universe is vast, and there are many dimensions.

2. Some beings or entities are able to cross from dimension to dimension and/or to send objects from one dimension to another.

3. There are naturally occurring places in the world where it is easier for those beings to pass back and forth.

4. There are human-made places in the world where turmoil, pain, and trauma have created paranormal hotspots.

5. Negative energy is part of existence, along with positive energy, much like yin and yang. You cannot have one without the other. The goal is to keep them in balance as much as possible.

6. When we encounter the paranormal, it is an opportunity to question how we are living and to work toward enlightenment and clarity of purpose.

I feel immensely blessed to have witnessed so many instances of the paranormal and to help the people involved feel heard and seen. I am grateful for how each paranormal event has brought me closer to the truth and to the deep meaning of the world. So much life has occurred on earth, and though life feels so fleeting, the energy of all those lives, whether human or animal, still exists. We live with and among those energies, which we sometimes experience as hauntings or simply as heightened energy.

But we also live in and among other worlds, which are stacked against ours, taking up space that we think we're the only ones to inhabit. Sometimes, though, we get a glimpse of the vastness of the universe and the endless infinity of existence.

Years after my final Bigfoot case, I was driving near Wheatfields Lake, north of Navajo, New Mexico, and northeast of Canyon de Chelly, in the area of my first beat as a Navajo Ranger. It was winter, and snow lay heavy on the ground and was still falling, a beautiful white against the rugged terrain and green pines. I drove along slowly, taking care in the snow. Suddenly, a tall, broad-shouldered, brown-haired creature crossed the highway ahead of me, moving from the left to the right across the empty, snow-covered highway, its fur flecked with freshly fallen snow. At first, I thought it was a bear, but then I realized it was walking on two legs, loping confidently across the road like a human. I watched wide-eyed as it disappeared into the trees on the other side.

Heart pounding with excitement, I pulled over to the side of the road and climbed out of my patrol truck. There, in the snow where the creature had crossed, were the footprints that had become so familiar to me over the years: enormous, bigger than a man's, leaving deep impressions in the fallen snow.

Bigfoot had passed by, moving briefly through our world, on some business of his own whose purpose I may never know.

But I drove home with a sense of awe in my chest, the snow-covered world of the Navajo Nation suddenly as infinite as the heavens. Once more, I had caught a glimpse of the truth lurking beneath our day-to-day existence: The universe is much bigger and stranger and more wonderful than we can even begin to imagine.

But the least we can do is try.

EPILOGUE

FOR YEARS, THE CHIEF NAVAJO RANGER, LEONARD BUTLER, kept telling us he was going to retire, but he never did, always staying on for "just one more year." So, in 2017, when he called me into his office to let me know he had set the date of his retirement for the following month, I was genuinely shocked. But I was not at all surprised when he told me that I would be his delegated replacement. I had been the chief's go-to guy for a long time, and I had always assumed that he would want me to fill his shoes once he decided to retire.

I was happy to serve my community in this way, and at the time, there really wasn't anyone else willing to do the job. The department had dwindled to a mere fifteen commissioned Rangers. I knew I could fall back on my Incident Command training and years of running special operations to do a good job. I had the management and organizational skills required.

But a part of me knew that it wasn't really what I wanted to be doing. Running a department meant dealing in tribal politics, as well as interpersonal ones, and I had done my best to avoid politics for my entire career. Having watched my father and uncles navigate those fraught waters, I knew that politics was an arena I wanted to avoid, whether it was in my blood or not. I'd seen too much corruption, infighting, and abuse of power to want to participate in that world. Plus, dealing with budgets—or the lack thereof—was not how I wanted to spend my days.

But I dutifully took the job, despite not receiving any increase in pay. I continued to receive a sergeant's salary while performing the duties and responsibilities of the Chief Ranger for over two years, and to this day I have never received compensation. I was now responsible for the life and safety of each individual ranger, not to mention each and every Navajo citizen, visitor, and non-Navajo who called Navajoland their home. The job was exactly what I had expected—a huge responsibility, constant headaches, and far more internal bickering than I ever wanted to encounter. At the same time, I was becoming disillusioned with law enforcement. Seeing so much evidence of police brutality and corruption on the news disgusted and embarrassed me, and I was now certain that law enforcement was a profession that no longer represented what I stood for. So, when political machinations forced me out of the position of Chief Ranger, I was more than ready to go.

I was soon given the opportunity to work as an investigator in another department. I knew I could do the job, but I quickly discovered I was out of the frying pan and into the fire, dealing with even more conflict, dysfunction, and political infighting. I put forth my best effort and endured those difficulties for a year and a half before deciding that it was simply time for me to retire and enter another phase of my life. I made it out of law enforcement without any bullet holes in my body and without having to put bullet holes in anyone else's, though I certainly came close a few times. I had achieved the goals I wanted to achieve in law enforcement, I had done all I could, and now it was time for a new chapter in my life—literally: I started writing this book.

Because of my and Jon's work with MUFON on the Old Man and Satan Butte cases, we had become familiar with the MUFON's Phoenix office. They invited Jon and me to be guest speakers at their monthly meeting, which was a huge success—a sold-out presentation. It was

clear that Jon and I could fill a particular niche in the paranormal investigative world that no one else had been filling—sworn law enforcement officers who had investigated the paranormal in the course of our
duties. People were deeply curious about our work and started calling
us "The Real *X-Files*."

Around the same time, we were introduced to a guy who ran a UFO-
related publication called *Open Minds*, as well as a popular YouTube
channel. We drove to Phoenix and filmed an episode with him, which
was very popular and gained a huge following. Soon after, one of our in-
person conference presentations in Laughlin, Nevada, was recorded and
posted to YouTube. It drew millions of views within a couple of months.

After that, invitations started pouring in—both locally and across
the United States and even internationally. Peter Broughan, producer
for the movie *Rob Roy* (1995) and *The Flying Scotsman* (2006) came to
Fort McDowell in 2013, and upon seeing our paranormal presentation
he invited Jon and me to present at the 2014 Scottish Paranormal Festival in Stirling. We accepted, and I'm so glad we did. The whole experience was straight out of a dream. Exploring ancient castles, viewing the
Highlands, and eating haggis and fish and chips was beyond amazing.
Our presentation at the festival was a hit. After that, invitations kept
pouring in—from China, Australia, Japan, Greece, Greenland, and
New Zealand. People were excited about the work we were doing and
interested in what we had to say.

That's when Jon and I realized that the paranormal experiences
we had spent our careers investigating weren't limited to the Navajo
Nation. Rather, they were a universal phenomenon. We started seeing
correlations we hadn't known about before. For example, just like the
Hopi in our part of the world spoke of Little People, those in England,
Ireland, and Scotland spoke of Little People too. All over the world,
people were experiencing Bigfoot and UFOs and hauntings of their
own varieties. And we could help them.

All of this interest in my work took me by surprise, and like everything else related to the paranormal, it wasn't really something I'd gone looking for. As a self-proclaimed introvert who would be happy to stay at home reading or playing guitar, I never set out to be in the limelight. Jon at least had a family background in the entertainment industry and was a bit more prepared than I was for this kind of attention. But, for better or worse, we had opened ourselves up to sharing about the paranormal, and people came flocking in to hear us, as well as to share their own experiences.

We set up a dedicated email address, where people could email us to ask questions about the paranormal or get advice for paranormal issues they were dealing with. We did our best to respond to as many as we could, but our email *blew up*, as today's young people would say. I was amazed at how many people had encountered the paranormal, and how wide a spectrum of experiences existed.

Soon, we were asked to film with four or five different production companies for episodes on several different TV shows. Jon was a guest on *Ancient Aliens*, and we both appeared on *Unsolved Mysteries*, *Skinwalker Ranch*, the spinoff *Beyond Skinwalker Ranch*, and *Indians + Aliens*. I've also appeared on an episode of *Paranormal Emergency*.

We continued to present at conferences all over the United States. Wherever we went, people wanted to tell us their stories, which many of them had never told anyone before. There were Bigfoot sightings and extraterrestrial encounters and all kinds of hauntings. It was clear that people needed a forum and a safe space to tell these stories, which many of them had been traumatized by and felt afraid to share with others. We were glad to provide that for them.

Sometimes, we would still be pulled into investigations, done in an unofficial capacity and usually on our own dime. Once, a producer Jon knew asked him to investigate paranormal phenomena happening in a woman's home. The family had been beset with skinwalkers that came into their house and at one point actually attacked her son. The poor woman was so stressed and afraid that her health began to suffer. Her family was ready to burn down their house rather than continue dealing with the frightening things that were happening there. They had to move out for their own safety. In the course of the investigation, it turned out that witchcraft was involved. Jon was able to offer his expertise and put the woman in contact with a medicine man who could help her. After that, the family's paranormal experiences stopped, and the woman later reached out to Jon to thank him. Even though I wasn't directly involved in this investigation, it felt good to know that the work Jon and I do was still continuing to help people.

Additionally, I realized that having a mission and a purpose in our retirement would help us too. So many law enforcement officers struggle with depression and substance abuse when they leave the force, and many don't survive even a decade into retirement. I suspect that the newfound lack of purpose in their lives is largely to blame. Jon and I now have plenty to keep us busy and useful. At the time of this writing, we have several different projects in the works, and more opportunities keep coming our way.

Opening myself up to a second career in the paranormal has afforded me all kinds of new experiences—travel, food, and people. While I was a ranger, I barely had time for hobbies or relationships or anything except work. So, in my retirement, I'm happy to try new things, meet new people, and see more of the world. After all, that's the inevitable outcome of learning more about the paranormal: It expands your view of the world and the universe, of humankind, and even of yourself. My career as a paranormal investigator in many ways is only just beginning, and I'm excited about all the things I don't yet know, the stories I haven't heard, the people I haven't yet helped.

A few years ago, Jon and I were in New Mexico, giving a presentation at a UFO conference. After the talk, we were standing in the lobby talking to conference attendees when a Native American woman in her late eighties or early nineties approached us. She was dressed in the traditional clothing of her tribe—the Jicarilla Apache. She wore an ankle-length skirt and tribal jewelry of beadwork and silver, her hair carefully arranged. She was crying as she embraced both of us. Jon and I reciprocated the hug as though we were her sons or grandsons. She thanked us for bringing our message to the public and giving people a safe place to share their experiences where they would not be shunned. She then described an encounter she had had with an extraterrestrial when she was a girl, one she had held close to her heart all these years, sharing with no one, not even her loving family. Her adult daughters and her granddaughters were with her, and their eyes widened in surprise as she spoke.

"Thank you," she said as tears ran down her soft grandmotherly face that had endured so many trials, tribulations, and hardships over many, many years. "Thank you both for letting me know that I'm not alone and I'm not crazy."

It was a sweet experience, but it was also sad. In that moment, I realized that so many people have had paranormal experiences they've kept hidden, waiting for a perfect moment to share them—a moment that for many will never come. They will carry that heavy burden for the remainder of their lives. But Jon and I had helped to give this Native American grandmother her moment, and she walked away from the conference unburdened.

That is exactly why I do what I do, and it is a role I am honored to fill. As I look into the future, I see many more opportunities to spread awareness, share the truth, and help people. For me, paranormal investigation is less about what's Out There than what's right here in front of us: a chance to connect with and help one another and to do our very best to make our world a better, kinder place than it was the day before.

ACKNOWLEDGMENTS

I OWE A DEBT OF GRATITUDE TO A GREAT MANY PEOPLE throughout my entire life who led me to reach this point to author a book:

Our dear Grandma "Vi" Viola and Bonnie, Lois, Bernis, Jennifer, Terry, Carmen, Gene, Sue, Russell "Rusty," Bill, Diane, Angela "Ang," Jacque, Jessica, Kelly, Grace, Kellie "Snookie," Vickie, James, Barry, Jalaina, Carla, Edgar, Rose and William Dahozy, Vincent, Bertha, Virgil, Valerie, Bertina, Shea and Margaret, Grandma Lillian "Lilly," Leo Milford, Irene, Sandra, Vivian, Kathleen, Harley, James, Carrol, Delores, Carl, Eugene, Elmer "Emo" and Julie, Robert, Erwin, LaDonna, Earl, Grace, Tony Sr., Lillian, Vera, Brandon, Gerald, Dwayne, Tony Jr., Ciara, Hyliah, Steve, Ron, Joy, Aaron, Arlo, and the following families: Dahozy, Watchman, Silversmith, and all the family members, children, and grandchildren of those above.

Many, many close friends and their families: Jonathan "Redbird" Dover, DeAnna, Eveline, Gerald "Dixie," Matilda "Renae," Marianne, Don, Stacey, Rose, Jim, Chuck and Vicki, Chuck and Nancy, Bob and Margie, Joshua, Chief Leonard G. Butler, Michele and Jim, Tim, Peter, Nick, Dusty, Brenda, Hoss, George, and Lorrie Sarafin's beautiful and inspiring music.

All Navajo Rangers, past, present, and future; Navajo Public Safety and Navajo Police; all law enforcement, EMS, firefighters, and public safety personnel everywhere—a big thank-you for the job that you do! And the many Navajo Nation employees; and all Native American and First Nations Peoples.

All "Paranormal Rangers" fans and those interested in the science of paranormal and supernatural phenomena.

All the music groups and artists that supplied the soundtrack to my entire life. (Thank you to my mother for my lifetime music appreciation class.)

All my classmates from Peggs Elementary School, Tahlequah Junior High and High School, Haskell Indian Junior College (University), Fort Lewis College, and the University of Arizona.

I extend a very special thank-you to the following people:

All the HarperCollins team: Mauro, Andrew, and those behind the scenes in editing and design, and those who worked to create an amazing cover. Erica—I could not have asked for a more amazing, talented, knowledgeable, inspiring collaborator and all-around wonderful person; I was so blessed to be able to work with you. I'm also appreciative of my literary agent, Frank, who was very understanding and supportive throughout the entire process. Thank you to my good friend Robert, who was always there throughout my career, lending his friendship, support, guidance, and best advice.

I owe a great debt of gratitude to so many people, but I'm not able to list everyone, or this would be several pages long. I do love and appreciate each and every one of you.

And one last great big thank-you to my Creator, Jesus Christ, and the many guardian angels and ancestral protectors who have watched over me and my family, and have kept us safe over the years.

INDEX

ABOUT THE AUTHOR

The son of Cherokee and Navajo parents, Stanley Milford Jr. spent most of his childhood growing up between rural Oklahoma and the Navajo Reservation in Arizona. He graduated from Haskell Indian Junior College in Kansas and attended Fort Lewis College in Colorado and the University of Arizona in Tucson, Arizona. It was while he was in Tucson that he was asked to return to the Navajo Nation to work as a Navajo Ranger. Stan graduated from the United States Indian Police Academy at the Federal Law Enforcement Training Center in Artesia, New Mexico, and then worked continuously as a sworn law enforcement Ranger for over twenty-three years. During this time, Stan served as a Ranger Recruit, a Ranger, a Ranger Sergeant, and for two years as the Delegated Chief Navajo Ranger. Stan served as a department firearm instructor and as team leader for the Special Weapons and Tactics (SWAT) team charged to oversee all special operations. He was also commissioned as a Navajo Police Officer to work as a team member with the Navajo Police's Drug and Gang Task Force, which included working undercover with the FBI.

One of Stan's unique responsibilities as a Navajo Ranger was overseeing a section called the Special Projects Unit, alongside his partner Lieutenant Jonathan Dover. This section's primary role was managing cases and projects that were deemed critical, sensitive, or high profile in nature. These cases ranged from high priority investigations, dignitary protection, high risk detail, SWAT, and other emergency operations. One of the responsibilities of this unit was the investigation of cases that did not fit within everyday parameters of law enforcement or criminal investigation—paranormal or supernatural cases involving Bigfoot, UFOs, extraterrestrials, witchcraft, skinwalkers, ghosts, and hauntings.

In 2021, Stan decided he needed a change after serving for over twenty-three years as a Navajo Ranger. He then worked as the Senior Investigator for the Navajo Nation's White Collar Crime Unit and officially retired from the Navajo Nation in 2023, having served a little over thirty years in total for the Navajo Nation. Today, Stan and Jon Dover continue to investigate paranormal cases, all of which are now outside the official law enforcement capacity and on their own time. They frequently give presentations on the paranormal in the US and throughout the world.